Notes
Left
Behind

Other books by James Hayford

The Equivocal Sky

Our Several Houses

A Personal Terrain

Processional with Wheelbarrow

The Furniture of Earth

Four Women

At Large on the Land

Back the Same Day

Gridley Firing

Star in the Shed Window: Collected Poems

Uphill Home

James Hayford

Notes Left Behind

Last and Selected Poems

Oriole Books 1997 Burlington, Vermont

Note Left Behind

I'm going to take a book
Out by the pasture elm,
The one whose flaring crown
Commands our little realm;
There's a knoll there by the brook
Where I can lie and look
At the mountain and the town.

If I'm not back for chores
I'll be asleep — or lost
In reckoning the cost
To never come back indoors.

1950

Dedicated to my father —
poet, musician, teacher, friend —
these last and other favorite poems.

— Jamie

And to my love and partner of fifty-seven years.

— Helen

ISBN 0-9612652-1-3

"Our Steeple," "Pivotal," "Logical Conclusions,"
"The Secret Vale," and "The Law of Size" first appeared,
in quite different shapes and under different titles, in a
Christmas collection sent to friends in 1950. "Matter of
Poetry" first appeared in the collection for 1956.

"Spring Complaint" first appeared in *Yankee* magazine for
April 1937. "To Robert Frost" and "My Window" first
appeared in *Harvard Review* #3, Winter 1993.

The selected poems first appeared in *Star in the
Shed Window* and *Uphill Home*, both published by
New England Press.

Design: Claire Van Vliet and David Thorne.
Printed in the United States of America

For additional copies of this book,
please write the distributor:

The New England Press
P.O. Box 575
Shelburne, VT 05482

Contents

Acknowledgments

The publication of this book would not have been possible without the considerable and invaluable help of Paul Eschholz, English professor at the University of Vermont, and Betsy Eschholz. We are grateful also to Claire Van Vliet and David Thorne who worked on the design and production of the book, to Howard Mosher for his foreword, to Garret Keizer for his article from *Vermont Life*, and to Don Craig for his generous assistance in many ways. Thus Jim's literary executors — Howard, Garret, and Donald — go on loving and supporting him. Our gratitude goes to X. J. Kennedy and Robert Bruce, too, for their encouragement and advice. We have used three poems — "Persuaded," "Inner Part," and "Winter Night" — as Christmas greetings in the three years since Jim's death.

— Helen and Jamie Hayford

Foreword

Coming across James Hayford's final book of poetry is like discovering a bonanza vein of gold in a mine thought to have yielded the last of its treasures. Here for the reading are 149 new poems, along with a selection of some of the best previously published work, by one of New England's most beloved lyricists. Witty, clear as a bell, and remarkably accessible in an era when much contemporary poetry is unreadable, the poems in *Notes Left Behind* are cause for celebration, in Jim Hayford's Vermont and far beyond.

Like Jim's previous work, these poems are gloriously in touch with the natural world we all once lived in. They're full of elm trees with "flaring crowns," remote hill farms just large enough for a few cows or half a dozen goats (Jim loved goats, and for many years raised them), northern New England's sharply differentiated seasons, and weather of all kinds, from the eternally surprising first snowfall of the year to the fresh, "green smell" of an oncoming summer rainstorm. The tiny upcountry villages Jim lived most of his adult life in are here, too. With their ornate academies and libraries, comfortable steep-roofed houses, sprawling woodworking mills, and endangered railroads, the small towns in *Notes Left Behind* become a metaphor for the world at large.

Two or three times a week over the nearly 30 years that I knew Jim Hayford, he'd show me a new poem. "If you like, I'll say it for you," he'd offer, then read it aloud. As I read these poems, I could hear Jim's voice "saying" them: resonant, musical, slightly wry and speculative, wise. Above all, these are the writings of a great teacher conveying the wisdom accumulated by long experience and hard thinking.

Notes Left Behind is a gift left behind: a golden legacy for those of us who were fortunate enough to know and love James Hayford, and for the many new readers this splendid last collection should bring him.

HOWARD FRANK MOSHER

One

Old Tree

How many birds have you taken in, old tree —
How many sheltered from the summer sun
And even, somewhat, from the wind and rain?

How many nestlings have you seen fly free
And find first solo flight a victory won —
After the lonely fear of failing again?

1993

Our Steeple

The steeple in our scene
Has had a coat of white
And cuts against the green
Flank of our mountain height;

Tall belfry-arcs invite
The grateful eye aloft
And up the gleaming shaft
To revel in the light.

1950

Landscape with Figures

In every hollow with a village
Work-men and -women go about the tillage,
Not only of the gardens on the knolls,
But of the place's shy green souls.

1938

First Robin

In the top of a tree still winter-bare
At the edge of the pasture precipice
With the darkling valley at his feet —
The shining river, the road and rails —

The first robin sweetens the evening air,
Saying there is no life but this —
To swing on a twig and fondly greet
In deepening dusk one's hills and dales.

1964

A Distant Sea

Each spring our dooryard mud
Collects a snow-melt flood
Shaped like a distant sea
Whose bays and promontories
I've sailed along in stories.

1954

Spring Complaint

Just judging by the one I crossed on,
And by the way it jounced my load,
The country wives from here to Boston
Have laid their wash-boards in the road.

1936

Suddenly Green

So suddenly green
Our whole outdoor scene:

It's happened so fast
We're already grassed;

Our trees have grown skin
And birds have moved in.

What strikes me this spring
Is the speed of the thing.

1993

Village Farm

For my well-ordered buildings,
Repaired with my own hands,
And my well-ordered lands
(The total of my holdings,
Three-quarters of an acre)
I turn to thank my Maker.

Front lawn is sugar-bush;
Back yard is pasture, mowing,
Plum-grove, and ground for growing
Berries and beans and such —
A little farm in quotes,
The right size for six goats.

1952

Water Lilies

The water lilies on the stagnant swamp
Show crisp white shapes under gray ghostly cedars.
So beauty flourishes wherever it can.

1969

Pasture Enough

Pasture for goats
Who unlike cows
Just browse
And will not eat
Any stuff
Once trodden by feet —

Pasture enough
For such strict throats
Has to be wide
Enough to divide
So one half is browse
While the other half grows.

1974

Miser

One way to be a miser
Without one criticizer
Is cram your loft and shed
With hay and firewood.

1951

The Sound of Water

This meadow's haunted by the sound of water,
Not in the vulgar sense of spirits or spooks,
But so as to make the mower's purpose totter
In presence of the confluence of two brooks.

1949

Kindling

Look: sawing up stuff for kindling
I came on my late ax-helve
Which had been cut so spindling
I was obliged to shelve
It after one glancing blow.
Poor helve had been first to go.

Suppose this bucksaw frame
Had gone first: same old game —
I'd have laid it against the block
And fetched it a broadside knock.

So even tool eats tool
When we go after fuel.

1936

Trash-Pile

The mess to be disposed of if and when
Is nothing like the mess dumped there and then;

Order includes the pile where trash is put,
In sight, perhaps, but out from under foot.

1953

Between Trains

This railroad bridge I use
Most times I walk to town
Is empty between trains.

If I had any brains
I'd pick some place to clown
Where there'd be less to lose.

1980

Approaching Thunder

Sh! Up the valley I hear thunder.
The afternoon's turned hushed and black.
Twilight at four is such a wonder.
Perhaps we'd better be getting back.

See — up the valley there, it's raining.
Smell it already — that green smell.
The robins feel it coming, gaining —
They shout let it come on, pell-mell.

Oh, that cool breath will blow it nearer.
Flash — that was close — and closer yet.
Each leaf turns up a flashing mirror.
Splash! Get inside or you'll get wet.

1953

Credit Rating

I'm known at the bank
As a pretty good risk —
In fact quite a crank
About being brisk
To pay what I owe.

They know I'd be good
For a loan to buy wood —
Or borrow real dough.
I did, years ago.
But not lately, though.

1954

Twelve Dollars

I think I'm rich if I have twelve dollars
From teaching as many piano scholars,
All of it past due on bills
For lights, insurance, fuel, pills —

But minding what must soon befall it
Spoils all the fun of a swollen wallet.

1952

Street Scene

Some carry solitary shame
Imperfectly concealed,
And might well suffer public blame
If something were revealed.

Strange faces that we look into
Might rather we kept out:
We might suspect, we might see through,
And raise the dreaded shout.

1952

Still Vulnerable

No choice I ever made but still I make
Walking in thought the road I didn't take,
Attempting still to have and eat my cake;

Walking in rain a midnight street somewhere
Still carrying my self-made load of care,
No blame I ever bore but still I bear.

1966

Not Anybody's Son

Not till you've buried all your fathers
And are no longer anybody's son
Will you be wholly free to father
Your own child, or anyone.

That leaves just God whose love's expressed
In being possessive and possessed.

1966

Mystery Story

Crouched in your hiding place
Just off the railroad track,
You quickly turned your face
And showed me your plaid back,
As if to say:
I have seen you
In case you may
See me;
I do not care
(Or is it dare)
To see
Whether you do.

Should I have called, Hello,
What are you doing there?
And tried to get you talking,
Or (as I did) kept walking?
I wonder as I go.
Now I shall never know —
And you will never know.

1953

The Mystery of Day

I've hunted everywhere inside
Where anything might try to hide:

Behind the doors and taller chairs
And underneath the beds upstairs;

In a closet dense with dangling belts
I heard a chuckle somewhere else;

On tiptoe, fingering the wall,
I heard a footfall in the hall;

I turned the knob and let it squeak —
The hall was empty, bright and bleak.

The mystery of day all right
Is how its shades keep out of sight.

1953

The Unanswered Bell

Retreating on tiptoe from the unanswered bell,
The parties on both sides of the front door
Each wonder what the other wants of him,
By ringing, by not answering the ring.

The one outside wonders if he is watched
From the obscurity behind the curtain —
The only safe assumption is that he is.

The one inside wonders if he was watched
Coming in, and thus is known to be inside.

And which is better off, the one outside
In the public innocence of day, observed,
Or the one inside unseen but able to see,
Alone with his supposed misanthropy?

1962

An Inner Part

Out burning rubbish in the mild
Dim winter Wednesday afternoon,
I watched the smoke float up, and smiled
And hummed an inner part, in tune.
The mill whistle at three o'clock
Released the help to snack and talk.
The work of the world was getting done,
It seemed, not wholly without fun.
In embassies at capitals
Opponents talked. The principals
In love affairs sat up and smoked.
Porters and taxi drivers joked.
Ambitious people calculated.
Men in their studies contemplated.
I watched my fire burn and waited
Till I could go write down this song
About us all getting along.

1959

Our Mountains

What difference do our mountains make
That might not be out there at all
In the darkness round the meeting hall?

Rocky and sharp are the views we take
As members of the P.T.A.:
Our mountains show in what we say.

1955

Backyards

Along our village street
With only trees to screen us
Our backyards reach and meet —
Till darkness drops between us.

1977

Ship's Light

All through the daylight hours
Her life is part of ours;

Her house below the street
Helps make the town complete.

But nights her light might be
A ship's light out at sea.

1971

Free Library

The tiny village library
Still bills itself as free —
Two hundred books, or three —
Zane Greys and Harold Bell Wrights.
Suppose one of these nights
Some citizen were lost
For lack of Robert Frost?

1966

After Dark

What do you do in this town
After the sun goes down?

The grocery stands dark
Across the dim-lit park,

Appliance store and bank
Dark too on either flank.

Still, the bar shows a light,
Library's open tonight,

And so's the skating rink.
Here's what you do: you drink

Or read or skate — all three,
Perhaps, consecutively.

1973

What To Leave

I ask myself what public monument
I'd leave if I could be munificent:

School? Library? No, let's say theater,
Where every scene would speak to every sense
About the tragi-comic consequence
Of natural difference of character.

Of course I won't be leaving any stages;
I'll have to leave some drama in my pages.

1955

First Snow

Blanketing fields that lately were bare brown,
Let this soft midnight snow bring blessings down
On all the people in the little town.

1988

The Jones Library at Orleans

One building that I pass
Is such good brick and glass
As to content my eye
And please most passers-by
In this plain village where
Real architecture's rare.

1985

Leaves Falling

Leaves falling open our view
Through many a vacant tree
To the town's one avenue:
In winter we can see
How Main Street people do.

1973

Acceptance

Summer is over now
And this is the last night;
Shall we know how to bow
And say All right, all right,
We had our hour of sun,
Knew we were having it,
And can allow the one
To count as infinite?

1963

In the Wings

All fall we feel old winter
Just waiting in the wings
To bring us what he brings
From badlands known as hinter.

1991

All Saints

In the woods on All Saints morn,
Windless, mild for November,
I halted to remember
Grandparents, classmates, friends,
Our three who died when born;

While to the north, where the railroad bends,
As if to help me mourn,
A train wound long its lonesome horn.

1950

Death in the House

One cannot close a room
Because someone died there,
Or soon there'd be no home
With any room to spare
For company to come.

1951

For Whom the Bell?

No less in the dead watches of the morning
Although no car approach to need its warning
The automatic bell clangs at the crossing:

The one-o'clock, the two-o'clock is passing.
The wheels of wholesale trade incessant turn.
Great worlds continue while small worlds adjourn.

1952

Sleigh-Ride

The college had a sleigh-ride,
A buffalo-robe-and-hay-ride.

We'd ride a ways, then walk
To get warmed up and talk
Together — young folks sing
So loud on such a thing.

The full moon cast the wood
In meshes on the road.

1953

Winter Night

Luxurious long winter night,
You give me time to rise and write
A new poem or repair an old,
Before returning to delight
In dark and cover from the cold.

1992

The Unplayed Concert

Play a Mozart concerto?
Too bad I just don't dare to.

Nor do I have the technique
To make Beethoven speak.

But I spend late years sighing
For want of early trying.

1987

Mail-Train

Outside the glass the first snow-flurry
Is making the meadow indistinct,
But country and city still are linked:
The mail-train still will hurry.

I may yet hear the poem I sent
Has been found fit to print.

1950

Two

Real and Free

A poem should be
Both real and free
To excel reality.

1982

Right Words

Right words in the right order
Set down for good on paper —
Oh, this has been our study
Since the first hieroglyph:
We've kept poetry tidy,
If also rather stiff.

To loosen it a little
We've tried letting it prattle;
But look, alas — the attic
Filling up twice as fast
With matter no less static,
And far less fit to last.

So back to pruning: shave it
If you intend to save it:
Don't let it ramble on,
Don't let it wander off;
Brief speech, and then begone,
Causing a sigh, a laugh.

1962

Matter of Poetry

Matter of poetry
Is instants of coming-to-be:

Love when it first is spoken,
Faith when it first is broken —

Of wholes, these parts in token.

1955

Acting as King

Let your eye see
And your hand start to shape
An actuality,

And you cannot escape
Acting as king —
Pronouncing, sentencing.

1966

Finality

A poem may have an air
Of rough finality —
Like saying There,
That's that
(Hands go spat-spat).

1993

Side-Spinners

Spin horizontal cable?
Like spiders, poets are able:
Explorers who would try

Crossing from solid ground
To country yet unfound
Can brave the abyss thereby.

1966

Material Wings

If I were qualified for flight
Would I still think I had to write,
Or would flight be my whole delight?

The man who lacks material things
Is apt to be the one who sings:
Flyers command material wings.

1959

Fully Human

Most poems are fully human —
They bear fatal defects;

Still, some show more acumen
Than even the poet expects:

These he collects.

1952

High Beauty

Of high beauty the first
Property may well be
Unreachability:
We're meant to thirst.

1959

Second Thought

In order to succeed
A poem may need
A second thought
To couple with the first
And generate a burst —
Of strangeness, like as not.

1973

Blame and Credit

What I have said is mine —
I take the blame and credit —

But that I saw and said it
To fortune I assign,

And to my gentle wife
Whose warmth has blessed my life.

1950

Day of Prayer

So dull and gray
A winter's day,
I'll plan to stay
Inside and pray.

And pray for what?
That doors won't shut
Until I've got
Some poems shaped up —

And, maybe, placed
Where they should last
Among those classed
American best.

1971

Outsider

Till someone of importance says "important,"
I can expect to stay unnoticeable;
Qualifications won't be what get me in
Unless I catch the attention of a Member.

1957

Analytic

Someday a doctoral critic
Is going analytic
And reason me away.
But that won't turn me gray;
By then I'll *be* away.

1950

To My Angel

You, angel who have helped my verse,
Dear resident guardian and nurse,
Let me acknowledge you and take
My turn in time to do the same
For some touched inarticulate
Aspirant keeper of the flame
Whose warmth makes magic man's estate.

1963

Three

To Samuel Babcock Booth

I spent time on my knees when young
While Mass was being said or sung;
This was because you, Bishop Booth,
Dear mystic Bishop of Vermont
And my great mentor in my youth
Embodied all I'd come to want.

1993

Rowboat

Its oars and oarlocks gone,
The rowboat rides the lawn
As a planter full of phlox —

As inappropriate
As burying its late
Oarsman in a waterproof box.

1973

Dream House

"Bay window, fireplace, and winding stairs —
These were the three desires
I mentioned in my girlish prayers."

1955

My Father's Friends

The men my father called
Not rich but well-to-do
Were heavy men and bald
Whose houses, heavy too,
Were usually brick-walled.

The men my father admired
Were men with nimbler wits
Than trade really required —
Unlike him, graduates
Of places domed and spired.

1960

Platform Talk

Contrary to common personification,
A train's not a *she* in the train station:
Trainmen say *they* — They're late, or They're due —
Thus rightly counting the crew — and you.

1949

Personal Beauty

Look anywhere:
In any rotting street
A haloed face
Or a body's moving grace
Inflicts defeat
On the devouring air.

1967

Man in Love

Ah yes, your fault was loving all too much
Beauty that was not always yours to love,
With love that would not only look but touch
And hold what it was so desirous of.
Restraint and modesty were gifts you lacked
When perfect beauty was in view; then all
Your body's virtue bade you rise and act
Before the vision passed beyond recall.

Of course this was no way to win the respect
Of those whose blood was slower and more chaste,
Whose lidded watchfulness was to detect
The moves their neighbor made in loving haste —
    And hoard this evidence against the day
    It could be used to give the man away.

1962

Alcoholic

When my old friend, now hurt by drink,
Tries to avoid me in the store,
At first I ask how can he think
I think myself superior.

And then I know: I'm not hurt, yet;
I'm still what's called respectable.
He feels he has to show regret
At having got so pitiful.

How can we ever again touch,
He drinking daily deeper shame,
I something else, not better much —
In either case, more of the same?

1955

Dear Boy:

The only man that ever called
Me "dear boy" was a Greek man, dark and bald,

Who at my college sold us hot dogs — gave us,
When we were broke and couldn't pay to save us.

He didn't know our names, but had to call
Us something, so "dear boy" did for us all.

He knew we'd pay sometime — most of us would;
He trusted boys in ways no father could.

1944

The World Moving

With curtains parted and the blind pulled up —
Its slats, she says, are prison bars —
The old woman at the window counts the cars —
Where can so many people have to go?
It's not that she does not approve —
She likes the world to be on the move —
What would she have to watch if it should stop?

Just let me out of here for once, she says.
If only I could ride to Rutland, say,
What wouldn't I see!
The shapes of snow on the roofs of barns
Where the wind has sculpted it,
The shapes of bare black elms by the road
With their blue shadows stretching out —
To have the world moving again
Because I was moving through it!

1962

32

My Father's Party

Fifty red roses on the desk
Denote the end of a grotesque
Lifetime devotion
To a cool-hearted corporation —

And banishment from this bright stage
To the gray privacy of age.

1952

Child Playing Late

Child playing late
Inside the dooryard gate
While the fall sky goes cold
And gray as slate
And all the hills burn gold —

Dear child, your fate
May never hold
A circumstance more fortunate
Than this encircling fold,
Half slate, half gold.

1959

Stomach Pill

What, sell my stomach pill
With models who *look* ill?
No, no, they must look well.

Come, say it as you should:
You mean they must look good.

Good-lookers are what sell.

1990

Beginning to Be Beautiful

"I haven't hurried to tell you this, my child,
But you're beginning to be beautiful."

"I am? What then?"

                    "You'll grow more beautiful."

"If I begin, does that imply I'll end?"

"I hope not, but that may depend."

                           "On what?"

"On what this kind of growing does to you."

1972

The Red Coat

Loving was once to note
In all the crowd on skates
Only the one red coat —
And its successive mates.

1952

Helen in Her Rural School

"Will you read to us now?"
"Let's see" — this with a smile-
"I asked for quiet, and how
Did you act, back awhile?"

No answer. "You told me no.
Don't shake your heads, you thirds,
You fourths in the back row.
Acts are the loudest words."

1950

Batter's Box

Three chances to hit the ball—
Just three strikes and that's all?

Oh, you'll get more than those—
That's more than just three throws:
You'll get two strikes and three balls
As per the umpire's calls.

Bad throws are balls; good, strikes.
Batter picks ones he likes—
And if no strike takes place
They give him a free base.

What guarantee is there
That pitchers will play fair?
You have the umpire who
Has power to see they do.

So rational the frame
We give the national game.

1990

The Face of Authority

The young-one playing cop
Holds up his hand for Stop:
Then, not content with gesture
To keep us in our place,
Puts on the legal vesture
Of the tough poker face—
As if it took a jaw
To represent the law
And put rough types in awe.

1953

The Snooty

They carry their noses
In such studied poses,
What should be their faces
Are only blank spaces.

1991

Married Looks

The happy couple laughing and talking
Are having such a good time walking
You think they certainly aren't married:
The married looks are blank or harried.

1966

The Tranquil Sweeper

Moving the row of rubbers
To sweep behind the door
The seventh time this week,
She might well curse the lubbers
Who wore them in to leak
All over her clean floor;
But she in fact is glad
A place is to be had
Where footgear will be warm
Next time it comes to storm.

1951

Short Walk

Old one, your walk is short these nights —
Down the dark street a little ways,
Then back where you left on the lights
That show you what you look at all your days.

1967

A Quiet Man

How often a quiet man's repute
Lags his accomplishment:
A modest work may stir much cry
If its maker seek advertisement,
Or may be almost mute
If the man be shy.

1964

Student Audition

Me in the audience
She won, not by her skill
At playing on the flute,
But by the liveliness
And earnest confidence
With which, ignoring dress ·
And person, not quite pretty,
She offered up her ditty
Devotedly and shrill:
The word for her was cute.

1956

Dear Gertrude Stein:

The one time you addressed me
(The only time we met)
In language bold and breezy,
"Young man, may you find life easy,
But not too easy,"
I never shall forget;
You practically blessed me.

1950

Four

Bird's-Egg

In this frail empty half a bird's-egg shell
Still spattered from the chick's
Excretions and exertions,
I hold a touching instance of how well
One can design a small receptacle.

1992

An Up-Late Bird

From high in a still leafless tree
An up-late bird upbraided me
For threatening her brood
By walking in her wood.
I said I came for solitude,
But stood for brotherhood . . .

She stopped me where I stood.
I withdrew silently.

1978

A Robin's Work

By eight a robin's morning's work
Is already half done
Since he began at four o'clock
Before the sun.

How many worms must one unearth
To do a robin's-worth?

1993

On His Side of the River

A dog that chases cars
Is an ill-mannered cur,
And I don't know any cure.

One dog, at a place I pass,
Has found a way to give chase
Without even coming close:

A river wide though shallow
Divides this clever fellow
From the cars he aims to follow,

And I say, Good dog, Rover;
Chase back and forth forever—
On your side of the river.

1950

Young Dog

A young dog joined me in my walk,
And though I could have had more talk
With him if I had known his name,
I clucked and made him other pledges
To keep up my end of the game.

He leaped a wall, explored the hedges,
And rattled the leaves in meadow edges;
He boldly nosed his yapping kind
Before whose onrush I may quake,
And left them pacified behind.

So well-born confidence will take
A youth in hand who has his way to make.

1935

The Banished Cat

Dear cat who slept between our feet,
Now banished from the electric sheet,
We miss your little body curled
Beside us in the dark of the world.

1952

Query About a Horse

Do you suppose he has the sense
That middles can be too immense,
And that's what makes him keep the fence?

Or does he simply like to stand
At his own farthest limits and
Look out across a foreign land?

1962

Indifference to Wet

The creatures in their stalls
Inside the open barn
Don't seem to mind the rain
As all day long it falls;

And I whom storms upset,
Who'd like things cozier,
Am comforted by their
Indifference to wet.

1954

Goat-Nature

Whoever has had dealings
With animals — say goats —
Wonders about their feelings:
Seeing them stand all day
So patiently in stables,
He wonders, are they bored?

They plainly enjoy oats,
Banana peels, and hay,
Rose bushes, strange to say,
And glue from tin-can labels.

They plainly fear the vet,
Whose needle denotes bleeding,
And they hate getting wet.

Yet though you're late for feeding
You never see one sulk
Or not let down her milk.
They take what they can get
From people and the Lord —
They want what we afford.

1954

Room to Flourish

Why is it carrots thinned
Droop some time as though stunned
By force of rain or wind?

The ones the fates thus cherish
Were propped by those who perish
To give them room to flourish.

1953

The Law of Size

As nature is our source
And constant reference,
We follow nature's course

Where size determines force:
Big stars and governments
Hold small ones in suspense.

1949

Stars

O stars, I never know
Whether you're for
Me or
No.

1968

Five

To Robert Frost
A Letter Never Sent

Sir, nothing would grace my life
Like having your pocket knife
(When you are through with it)
To open a bag of oats
Or slit a friend's epistle,
Or cut me a willow whistle
Out back by the brook in spring:
I owe some pastoral notes
To you who taught me to sing.

If my bid seems premature
It's because I'd like to be sure
Of forestalling the museums
Who'd enshrine you with Te Deums.
I'd keep you warm in my pocket
On a guard-chain like a locket;
I'd keep you keen with use.
This interest is my excuse.

Let them exhibit your pen.
Fact is, your poems are whittled:
They're shapely, they stand up well-victualed,
And speak with deep voices like men.
You came out of the woods to the schools
Debating unto themselves,
And handed them handles and helves
To get hold of — you gave them tools.

I'm not much on tradition
As touching crowns and thrones,
But the little a poet owns
Beside his pure ambition
Deserves direct transmission
From hand to laboring hand.
Such, sir, is the petition
Of another who works the land.

1952

Thoreau

"Thoreau," the young instructor muses,
"A man who knew life's proper uses,"
Assigns a chapter more of *Walden*,
Draws a neat parallel with Mauldin,
"The world is too much with us" quotes —
The class include it in their notes.

"What about that, sir?" a boy demands;
"You think we ought to chuck our hands,
All of us, and go live in huts?"
How to explain, the instructor broods,
That the best of men have times and moods —
But old Thoreau will have no buts.

"Well — yes," he says, "Ideally yes.
To live well is the one success —
But you alone can save your soul."
What are you doing saving ours?
The unsaid question haunts his hours.
Loving Thoreau the less, he'd be
No teacher; loving more, he'd flee.
Teacher, teacher, how to be whole?

1950

Brother Sebastien at the Organ

Brother Sebastien? In the chapel. Come.
The window on the cloister may be open —
Usually is in weather warm like this.
Sh — there he is. So soft. Mood pastoral.
Let's sit here on the bench and listen to him.
The flute stop on the Swell in 12/8 time.
It's "He shall feed His flock" — yet unlike Handel.
Sebastien takes a motive from the Mass,
Quite often, and departs from there, for parts
Unknown. His meditation is by music.
His discipline is musical restraint —
He dawdles on his way to smell a flower —
Soprano do; alto re, mi, fa, mi,
Fa, mi, re, mi — Well, let's get on with it.
Perhaps he's strolling still in pastures green,
But now he lifts his eyes up to the hills
From whence — my, listen now — soprano fi —
He loves chromatics — French composers do,
Specially organists — now up to si —
Surprising — where can he be going — ah —
Neat, eh, that altered chord — anything else,
One feels, would have been commonplace —
And now the vista opens out — *voila* —
One has arrived somewhere, for just a moment.
Onward and up? No, he is going to rest
Awhile and contemplate what he has seen.
Will he be able to find that path again?
Is he rehearsing one of his finished works,
Or improvising only for the joy,
Or possibly composing something new?
I said his discipline is musical
Restraint. Well, his objective is the reverse —
Musical abandon. He begins
By playing the organ, but he ends, he says,
With the organ playing him. So God comes down.

1958

When Prexy Died

Too bad about old Stanley, eh? Sudden.
Not that I ever really liked him much —
But still, he leaves a hole. Who's going to fill it?

I've been appointed Acting President.

You have? You're kidding!
                              Farnham called from New York,
Oh, half an hour ago. They'd met — by phone,
I gathered — some key members of the Board.

And handed it to you! Well, happy landings.
The dear old college wasn't skipperless
For long now, was it? What time did Stanley die?

Soon after midnight.
                 You were there?
                                Bess phoned me,
Quarter after eleven. I went over.

You were quite thick with Stanley. Did he say —
Had he picked you?
                   He was unconscious then.

Never came to again? So you don't know.
Bess said he'd spoken to Farnham about —
                                You?
Expressed a preference — or so she thought.

I might have known. He didn't like me much.
I never hid the fact I didn't like him.

You never hid the fact you don't like me.
What'll you do, resign?
                    You crazy? You
Haven't got the permanent appointment, yet.

You mean to make a fight for it.
                         Damn right.
Well, happy landings. May the best man win!

1964

The Fighter

I fought to save your father his good name
When he would have brought all of us to shame.
I went to the directors of the bank
And made them — hear that? — made them hide the blame.
For what he has now, he has me to thank.

But for the force of my persuasion, they'd
Have brought the charge against him. But I made
Them, made them listen: "Only give me time;
I'll see that every cent of it's repaid."
I saved us from the ruin of his crime.

I took up dressmaking to pay his debt.
I've kept our home together by my sweat,
While he has sat and grumbled and took on.
And yet, despite all, I'd have no regret
If I could feel you'd love me when I'm gone.

1951

The World's Biggest Business

Here's all this air going to waste —
Nobody making a profit from it.
People pay to live in it, and move
In it, and send messages through it,
But do they pay to breathe it? No.
It's the last free resource. What's more,
It's inexhaustible. Oh boy!

Get Congress's permission to
Pollute it. That shouldn't be hard;
Factory stacks and automobiles
Already make a modest start.
But I mean really poison it —
A handful of cheap chemicals
Per day should do the trick. And then,
Sell everybody metered gasmasks,
And metered filters for the home —
So much per cubic foot consumed.

How will the people get the money?
Why, most of them will work for me.
Think of the manufacturing,
The distribution, the sales force,
The meter-readers and service men!
The masks and filters could wear out
Daily, or weekly — let's say monthly —
It wouldn't do to be thought greedy.

And then, of course, the foreign rights.
No nation would be civilized
Without it — think of the employment!
In case resistance should develop,
Attribute the pollution to
The Enemy. Why, Senator,
It would be un-American
To overlook such a source of profit!
Think of mankind fully employed
Earning the wherewithal to breathe!

1954

Forest Food

"I take it you're Aunt Ann," the squirrel said;
"I judged you were by your grey head,
And the way you always smiled.
The children said to tell you they're not dead,
Nor grown up, only gone
Further into the forest with some faun —
I don't know who. They left their acorn cups
And saucers here with me by this old oak.
You'll stay for tea, Aunt Ann?
Oh, surely you won't choke,
Not you. You know whoever sups
On forest food must be a child —
Or a child again."

1935

First Spat

"What is it makes you want to hurt me so?"
She wadded her wet handkerchief into
Her apron pocket.
          "There you go again.
You think whatever I do is aimed at you."
He turned to face her, half way across the kitchen.

"For one who doesn't aim, you make good hits."

He said, "What are you afraid of losing? Tell me."

"I'm not afraid of losing it. I've lost it."

"What?"
      "Just you."
          "Oh fiddle-dee-dee — I mean,
I'm sorry. You surprise me so — don't cry."

"Just you, and me, the way it used to be.
That's all I ever had, or ever will have.
You never want to be with me any more."

"Oh come now, I have things I have to do.
We both do. We must move, and change, and grow."

"Apart."
     "We couldn't sit forever on
Your mother's sofa, holding hands." He smiled.

"We have a sofa now." She almost smiled.

"And work to do before we make use of it."
He kissed her. "Now may I go start my chores?"

1952

The Missing Masterpiece

What has become of the great man's great book —
The one we've all been sure he must be writing —
The longer it took the better it would be?

That's what we've told ourselves as the years went by.
But now he's in his eighties and still no book —
Nor even articles in the reviews —
Those brilliant articles he used to write.
Not any more. Has he dried up? Can't be:
His conversation's still as sharp as ever,
Still critical of everything he reads —
Or sees — of all that's going on around him.
Is he just too critical of himself to write?
Does he dread being criticized by others?

That last is almost impossible to believe.
Perhaps he hasn't found the perfect subject —
The one nobody ever attempted before.

Then let him write a book about his search.
We seem to think he owes us a great book.

1977

Six

Architect

I used to think I'd be an architect —
Of Georgian homes and public halls —
Old buildings really, only with new walls —
Which both our schools of thinking would reject;

The antiquarian wants his antique —
That's really old — old style and substance too;
While the modernist wants nothing but what's new —
That's new all over — free-form, glassy, chic.

Still, some people, like me, who won't inherit
A stately place and can't afford to buy one,
Might like a new house with a mellow spirit
And moderate upkeep, if I could supply one.

1962

The College Architect

My failure — what, you haven't seen?
Right this way, down across the green.
We approach it from above now, do we not?
And that's what the trustees forgot.
For classic balance I gave it wings —
Low, flat, one-storey things
That on the brow of a rising grade
Would have set off my colonnade
Of slender Doric shafts.
That's how I saw it in my drafts.
But the powers chose a different lot.
From this approach, the wings look squat —
Like field-stone chicken coops, eh what?

1961

Brigham Academy at Bakersfield

Those rows of windows through the lane of trees
Along the common — the Academy's —
The settling brickwork of the towered front,
The spreading cornices, the peeling paint:

Peter Bent Brigham's ghost must surely frown;
To rear this edifice in his native town
He brought his Boston architect and crew in.
Hard — nay impossible — to tear it down.

Regard it as the honored local ruin.

1966

The Loss Of St. Paul's, Burlington, 1971

Cathedral burning now,
You'll never be restored
Because no one knows how,
Wants to, or can afford.

Of course you'll be replaced
By a modernist essay
Whose future loss, at least,
Won't cause this much dismay.

1971

Random Angles

Nice thing about a college or a farm
Is how one building — say a dorm
Or tractor shed —
Will casually appear ahead
Unheralded
Between two others, set
At random angles, oddly met.

1976

Light in the House

Houses are full of holes
To let light in by day
And out by night,

So indoors has outsight
By day, and outdoors has
Insight by night.

1976

Scale

Right range has been the length
Of a cathedral aisle,
Which modern skill and strength
Could prolong by a mile.

Right reach has been the height
Of a cathedral spire,
Which modern methods might
Extend a half mile higher.

Right scale has been the size
That satisfied our eyes.

1984

Construction

Establish sound foundations,
Top them with solid sills,
Bridge two of these with parallel sleepers
In close ranks,
Cross these with double planks —
And this construction undergirds
The feet of men and herds.

1951

Modern Design

However angular and ambiguous —
Half ship, half summer hotel with tiered verandas —
The lake sidewheeler had a distinctive shape —
You could even call it a distinguished shape.
You'd never mistake it for a typewriter.
The "streamlined" ferry looks like a typewriter.

The steam locomotive looked like a — locomotive.
The diesel looks like an elephantine truck
With windshield wipers, which is what it is.
A house looked like a house, a school like a school —
All new buildings are indistinguishable
From cookie factories. I miss old shapes.

1970

Interiors of Sound

Music's interiors of sound
Pattern the hour plane or arching
As colonnades or arcades bound
A space with columns marching:

These heavy verticals or light,
These horizontals strict or loose
Serve both the hearing and the sight
In double residential use.

1950

Seven

Just Today

What we did yesterday,
What we must do tomorrow —

These givens guard the way
That brings us just today —

All we can own — or borrow.

1992

Our First Brevity

The first we knew of brevity,
Perhaps, was spooning custard up:
The sweeter 'twas, the sooner we
Got to the bottom of the cup.

1954

Say Yes

Accept the years that bring you strangeness — so
Receive what comes that what is gone may go:
Say Yes to the years; no good can come of No.

1957

Pivotal

The course of thought, being jointed,
Is frequently repointed
By a pivotal insight
That turns it left or right.

1950

A Certainty

One thing for sure about the young
Who are so bold
In saying everything we've done was wrong:
They will, if they live long
Enough, also grow old.

1964

What Needs Doing

What needs doing is plain
To any orderly brain:
Find who has what and who lacks what,
And each trade part of what he's got.

Someone with proper power
Could set this up in an hour.

1957

Troubles

The trouble with a dream,
It tends to be extreme.

The worldly are the wise
Because they compromise.

The trouble with a deal,
It may buy just one meal.

1957

Humanunkind

Man is the cruellest animal.
If you don't know that you don't know much.
That's where I start whenever I teach:

Man is the cruellest animal.
Not that I carry on or preach;
I simply say what you can't impeach,

That he's the cruellest animal.
I never said he wasn't rich
In good intentions and all such,

I just say he's the cruellest animal.
I know he sees himself, poor wretch,
As victim of a hopeless itch —

He's still the cruellest animal.
I'd give my waterproof gold watch
Not to be the son of a bitch.

1963

Learning to Fake

How early we learn to fake
Bad pain or sad neglect
To claim undue attention,

And how late we forsake
These tricks though their effect
May be large-scale dissension.

1990

Logical Conclusions

We're saved from going too far
Toward logical conclusions
By being what we are:
We're saved by our confusions.

We don't quite like the fruits
Of perfect clarity;
There are no substitutes
For clumsy charity.

1950

Correct Assumption

In choirs a strong soprano
For no especial bonus
Most always takes the onus
Of staying with the piano.

So social orders rest
On the correct assumption
Someone will have the gumption.
To be this soloist.

1951

Being Great

The great, as any great one knows,
Are more alike than we suppose
Because whoever greatly serves
Is in it, heart and head and nerves.

So, to define it for the nonce,
Greatness is absolute response,
Whether to pleasures or to dangers —
Which is why great ones seem like strangers.

1954

Something Else

Good work, you scientists
Who can predict
With logic sure and strict
That something else exists:

Your learning indicates —
Necessity dictates —
It has to be out there —
You know why, but not where.

1993

Manned by Boys

Too bad the world is manned by boys
Whose counter-feats of engineering
Keep everyone at odds and fearing
What the machines they use as toys
Seem sure to bring — the final noise.

1957

Autobiography

There was a time I did not think it odd
To speak, as though he were a friend, to God.

Finding this set me rather far apart,
I turned to speak to other men, through art.

I still was talking to myself, it seemed;
Through politics I'd build what men have dreamed.

Indifference I'd met, but this was hate:
How men resist being rescued from their fate!

1938

Midnight Resolution

The madmen whom the blind elect
Planning no change until the planet's wrecked,

Here's my small contribution
Toward saving humankind: this resolution

Composed near midnight by the clock
At a farewell party on a steamship dock:

To stay around and help pick up the pieces,
And further the continuance of the species.

1938

Eight

Awaking

From datelessness to date,
From weightlessness to weight —

And what today demands
Of back and legs and hands.

1992

Whose Body?

My body acting up, I tell it Stop;
Whose body do you think you are? And it
Replies Not yours; I'm part of the great pool
Of bodies that are lent to human beings.
I'm only yours on loan — don't you forget.
Too bad if you don't like me; you can't swap.
But never mind — your lease is almost up.
They'll cart me off to the great pile of bodies —
Having first removed any re-usable parts —
Eyes, kidneys, heart — nobody'd want this face.
I'll melt back into the available store
Of new materials for future use.

1982

A Look Ahead

These days whenever I look ahead
I hope I shan't hate being dead.

1992

Man from Boy

Reviving in my bower
At midnight, dawn, or noon,
I had to know the hour —
It never was too soon:

What's going on without me,
Employments of what joy?
I must be up and about me,
Deriving man from boy.

1953

Comical

This time let me be meant
To comically
Succeed by accident
Instead of tragically
Fail by necessity.

1955

If I Weren't I

If only I weren't I!
What does the voice reply
When I bewail my curse?

Why, if you were not you
You might be someone worse.

1954

My Window

For a window on the world,
One that commands a wood
Across an open field
Does me a lot more good
Than one that has a view
Of a stylish avenue.

I get embarrassed when
I'm with successful men;
There is a kind of shame
In owning such a need
To make oneself a name —
It costs too much to succeed.

Not that I wouldn't like
To have my small gift known,
But let the lightning strike —
Don't try to call it down.
Renown is up to heaven:
Not to be gotten — given.

1962

Peculiar

No one's peculiar any more but me,
And I'm far less so than I used to be.

No longer do I care, or is it dare,
To be supposed exceptional or rare.

In these times an extraordinary man
Is apt to be thought un-American.

1962

Why Here?

What am I doing here —
As if here were the bottom,
Or pretty near.

I halted here one autumn
When it became clear
Half a loaf was better than none —
Or even a whole one.

I settled here for fear
I might not know enough to stop
When I had reached the top.

1955

Vocational Guidance

Never announce your aim
In life, never admit it,
Or when you come to hit it
You'll have to take the blame.

1951

The Secret Vale

Toward the low end of earth
Must lie the secret vale
Where worthlessness and worth,
Truth, untruth, female, male,

Live all unsorted — where
My mind like Bach's at ease
Among pure qualities
Is improvising prayer.

1950

This Tune

The way this tune runs in my head
And will not go away,
It must be that the joyful dead
Are singing it at play.

1933

Your House

Have you forgotten, Lord?
This used to be your house —
You built it, every board,
Then blessed it with your word,
And made its church your spouse.

You do remember, Lord?
You called us family
And gave us formerly
Your own first-born to board —
We nailed him to our tree.

You meant for him to die,
And save our souls thereby?
But we've kept killing, Lord;
We've killed until we're bored.
Return, or at least reply.

1962

Timepiece

New works riding my wrist
In glassed case square and flat,
You'll tell me to desist
From this and get to that.

1956

God Our Mother

Had God been seen as Mother
Rather
Than Father,

Would so many have been so sure
That waging war
Was what they were created for?

1984

When Ned Cursed God

When Ned cursed God and didn't die,
I had a right to ask God why.

I waited twenty minutes or so
And then inquired did He know.

When nothing happened by the third
Morning, I nudged Him: *Had* He heard?

I called Him: *Was* it His intent
That Ned receive no punishment?

Then, since 1 couldn't well kill Ned,
I took to killing God instead.

1970

Left to Myself

Left to myself I'd cease
And sit around at peace
In any handy hovel —
And contemplate my novel.

1954

Persuaded

I am persuaded
That everything will *be* all right
In that good night.
The power that let us love and write
And think and build
Has not been killed
Even though our faith has faded
And grown perplexed;
It will make sense for us of what comes next,
I am persuaded.

1993

Selected Poems

Nine

The Never-Last Outpost

Leaving the last outlying farm,
North for an hour through cedar swamp,
You may well come to a square made calm
And civil by the old plain pomp

Of elms drawn up on either hand,
Where a slender church reproves excess,
And a fiddle shapes a saraband
Against the immediate wilderness.

1938

Hard Water

These hard, sleek pebbles of the brook
Are the soul of water as a book
May be the soul of man: they hold
In permanent miniature the cold,
The impersonal, the wave, the fish —
Take one to pocket if you wish.

1942

The Winter Lamb

Hush now, have you not heard?
Born to the cutting cold,
The winter lamb comes furred —
A white ball slickly rolled,
Well-snouted, dour, absurd.
There in the littered fold
Its first unmuffled word
Is clamorous and bold —
Sleep easy, now you've heard.

1950

Business Obligation

World where ambitious men
Tread on each other's heels,
I can remember when
You taught me how failure feels.

Yet if a man resign
The world, he may repent,
And loneliness is a sign
Of self-imprisonment.

Tranquil to do my work
In neighborly isolation
Is to accept, not shirk,
My business obligation.

1949

The Light on the Mountain

Their light's no more than a spark
Under the mountain's head,
But when they go to bed
They leave the country dark.

What time is it? Not late —
The night is not far gone:
Forerunners of the dawn
Are in their beds by eight.

And all they prophesy
Is that cold light will break,
And country stretch and wake
To an equivocal sky.

1950

The Headstrong Sun

Inflamed, the headstrong sun
Surmounts the leaf-clad earth
Who circles him in passion
To bring her seed to birth.

What if a cloud's intrusion
Interrupt them in their noon —
We feel her sudden shiver
Along the mottled river —

Let what he drew from water
Thwart his perspiring eye:
He will but pore the hotter
And blot the streambed dry.

1949

Both Ways of Winning

In each divided inning
You take both ways of winning:

Conservative in the field —
How little can you yield?

But then at bat, let's go —
Let's spoil the status quo!

You want to be wild *and* tame
To win the national game.

1949

Forecast Tonight

Forecast tonight are fog and rain —
The rain begins. Our roof is tight
Except for one small place in the porch
Which will not worry us: we're all right.

Luxuriously we have two thousand
Square feet over us three and the cat;
The goats and pullets in the barn
Share their six hundred — no leaks in that.

But our thoughts now are out the window
Of our upstairs bedroom in Vermont
Where the radiance of our lamp is quenched
In dripping black: may none be in want.

Co-dwellers all along this seaboard,
Are your roofs sound, each several one,
Millions in all, as we come under
The common rain in unison?

1948

To the Float

To the float is only a hundred yards,
But dusk is making it look dimmer;
And see, no guards —
The two of us, no other swimmer.

True, one should trust it under one,
This cooling sheet of cobalt shimmer —
So cool a son!
I'll swim you out where the camplights glimmer.

1949

Style

As the cold currents of the brook
Render its sands and pebbles clear,
Just so does style in man or book
Brighten the content, bring it near.

1950

To Poets

Though much we do is done for us
By spirit or spirits anonymous
Who when received find avenue
To things we had not known we knew,
Still, most will be by our own hand
As we keep answering the demand
Of good in people and the land.

1950

Our Pond

Seeing it dazzle through dark boles,
You might think our pond reached to the poles.

The water slapping at the wharf
Churns into something much like surf,

And I won't find the slightest fault
If you fancy the inshore breeze is salt —

Nor be surprised if some dazzled dreamer
Should wake to the hail of a London steamer.

1952

The Scythe

At haying when I crop
My roadside in the sun,
Somebody's sure to stop
And show me how it's done:

"Let's see that scythe — stand back.
You want to swing her wide,
See — what *you* do is hack.
See — eas-y, let her ride."

At least the shade is cool
Where I once more, excused,
Am taught this is the tool
Men hate to see abused.

1951

Dark Under the Table

Most all of you good neighbors go to bed
As soon as it gets dark under the table,
And I would do the same if I were able —
Our daylight steps should earn our daily bread.
But there is no rest in my restless head,
And I must pass under every darkened gable,
Hearing a horse stomp deep within a stable,
Hearing a wakeful dog growl in a shed.

Under the summer moon the maples' shade
Buries our still street like a forest glade.
The emerald signal at the railway station,
Keeping us still connected with the nation,
Catches the steel of one expectant rail
That swerves to miss the moonlit mountain pale.

1952

The Church at Newark

The sermon with its gaps
Conducive to short naps
Suggests life was not planned
For us to understand.

The church, though, stovepipe-spanned,
Declares how sure a hand
Here utilized the inch
As though it were a cinch

To bend both stair and bench
Without the slightest pinch —
A plan without perhaps,
Apology, or lapse.

1951

The Trouble with a Son

The trouble with a son,
You never get him done.

There's always some defect
Remaining to correct,

Always another flaw
To disappoint his pa —

Who knows how imperfection
May suffer from rejection.

1952

My Dread

I don't know where I got my dread,
But something someone long since said
At supper must have filled my head

With visions of nocturnal dealings
Where men and women without feelings
Consorted under smoky ceilings —

Not all my sunshine intercourse
With honest folk has had the force
To touch this terror at its source.

1952

Matinee

Flakes falling and fallen whirl
Round a woman, man, and girl
Breasting the noonday storm
A mile from any farm.

When I pull up the car
And call out, Going far?
They're glad to get inside
And gladder still to ride.

"Aggie, she had no school,
So Fred, the perfect fool,
He says never mind the blow —
Let's take her to the show."

1952

A Game of One Old Cat

My cat grows old
And minds the cold.
No sooner out
Than he wants in —
And turnabout.
I never win.
But no great loss.
Such is the wage
We owe old age,
Which can be cross
As well as sage.

1952

A Moment in the Midst of My Time

I slipped at the corner of the barn
And put out a hand to save my balance —
And it may tax my narrative talents
To get to the upshot of this yarn:

The weathered clapboard felt so warm
I turned to look at it, amazed,
And left my hand there, either dazed
Or shaken from my dazzled norm.

What I saw was the arm of an aging fellow
In definitely seedy clothes,
Caught in a somewhat silly pose
With a barn in grey and a sun in yellow;

And there by the grace of God leaned I
A moment in the midst of my time,
A moderate man in a temperate clime,
Having once been born, having once to die.

1952

My Native Scene

How shall I put my native scene
In spring before it puts on green?
Over the field of tousled flax
The mountain is a distant blue;
The tree that unifies the two
Is penciled in in greys and blacks.

Notice its infinite refinement
Or praise its formidable strength —
I could do either at some length.
Why not do both in the same assignment?
That's how I'll take my native view:
Good songs blend opposites, both true.

1953

Great Sun

Great sun, source of the goodness of our sphere,
Whose setting is a heavy loss of cheer,
Your very power may cause you to appear
Capricious, as the times you burn too hot;
Your very evenness may seem unfeeling,
As when you failed us that day miles from here
In course of a wild quest for what was not —
But who accuses you of double dealing?

The little lights we of late years invent
To see by when we'd better be asleep,
What are they but excitements meant to keep
Our nights as well as daytimes discontent?
And what but your invariable dear
Disinterestedness is innocent?

1955

The Concluding Hour

In the concluding hour
From evening chores to bed,
The sky still overcast
From the receding shower,
The right word should be said
About the day being past —
How was it, slow or fast?
What if it were our last?

Away on top of the hill
Against the leaf-dark wood
Under the soft-lit sky,
The children are on high
Repairing the old tree house
In the great maple tree —
Hark, hear them shouting still?
When back of the barn I stood
And looked just now, I could see
A white shirt, or a blouse.

They will come down to bed
When the warm windless hour
Fails and the day is past
And I shall find you curled
In slumber by my side
When I come up at last
After the word is said
And I again have tried
Conclusions with the world.

1954

Address to Those Who Don't Go to Meetings

Address the college —
I, dressed formal?

First, I'm no scholar —
I'm short on knowledge —
I lack for a text.
And next,
I've mislaid my collar,
Which never felt normal.

Can't I in these clothes
Address me to those
Who don't go to meetings?

Greetings,
Lone farmers and fishers
And unemployed wishers
Who don't join the crowd
Because you're too proud
Of not being rich,
Or else haven't a stitch
And so aren't allowed;
You authorized hermits
And you without permits
Who'd hate to be named —

You think I've been tamed.
Oh no, there you're wrong.
I just half belong
To the social order.
I don't and I do.
I live on the border.
Ask them if they trust me —
You'll find they've discussed me —
They class me with you.

I join them from love —
Of lots of their ways —
And there's a bad phrase
To be guilty of.

Let me lay this before you:
You've a right to be wild.
So let them ignore you
And don't feel exiled.

1953

The Resident Worm
for Donald Ames Craig

The pitcher plant makes a living by
Enticing living things to die
In quest of ruinous delight.
It keeps an adjutant that thrives
On this rich harvest of lost lives —
A resident worm or parasite.

On the other hand, the goldenrod
Survives invasion by a worm
That dines upon its endoderm
And winters in a private pod —
An ugly but benignant cyst
That isolates the colonist.

So life is given and taken in ways
That are too hard for us to praise —
Inhuman is the word for God.

1955

Dark Portal

At my first approach to a covered bridge
As a child
When going to ride
Was a privilege,
The dark portal looked so small
Through the windshield of the truck —
It made me duck.
We must be too wide
And much too tall.

My father smiled.
"Don't worry, we'll fit;
We'll be the right size
When we get to the rise."
And we were, but the approach was exquisite.

1949

Handmade

Poems are still made by hand
So slow is the demand —
All somewhat different,
Each an experiment
In actual delight.
Not many turn out right;
Few households have a sound
Fresh specimen around.

1955

The Principle is Growth

Of moving immobility
The model is a tree.
Compliance, fixity,
The tree has both.
The principle is growth.
The essence is to live,
To stay put and yet give,
To sway and still not snap —
And what it takes is blood or sap.

1954

Law

Fear is the fatal feeling
That comes from seeing Law
Order its iron dealing:

Nobody ever saw
Nature or county court

Without inquiring why
Mercy is in such short
Supply.

1955

Snow in the Trees

Snow is a sleepy motion in the trees
That takes the eye with business ever witty.
And I suppose it's snowing in the city
Amongst the sheer rectangularities
Of light-shot business and apartment blocks
In avenues distinguished for their glitter.
Oh, I am neither envious nor bitter;
The city's fine, I would not change my walks.

I might be tempted to betake me there
If city folk were minded to produce
Elegance of equal or superior use
To, say, a Wren facade or a Mozart air.
It must be I still have the old-style notion
Our works should fill the air with cheerful motion.

1953

Christ Coming

Christ coming through split cloud
Unto his mother's womb
At the turning of the year
May not have seen the crowd
That took up every room
As anything to fear.

Later, leaving, lonely,
Suffering at their hand
By act of the elect,
He may have asked why only
The unsuspecting stand
Unanimously suspect.

1954

In My Great Content

In memory of all the days I've hated,
The featureless and lost, unnamed, undated
Days when I hurried through my work and waited

For some composing touch that would not come —
In memory of those, which I am from
As much as from the clear and venturesome —

I frame this tribute in my great content.
But for those days misshapen and misspent,
Should I have known what composition meant?

1957

Sky Pond

Far more susceptible are you, fair water,
Level and limpid, than the coarse dry land —
The sky's reflective and
Most filial daughter.

I should have lived where you are never frozen
And summer does not cost a winter's price,
Had not my fathers chosen
Seven months of ice.

1957

The Mirror of My Realm

In the corner back beyond,
Where the brook enters the spruces,
I have a little pond;
Its banks are smoothly lawned
And it has several uses.

The cattle come to drink,
A frog lives in the brink,
It is my swimming pool;
I take there what I think
Is the only sport that's cool.

On the cool grass I sit
At dusk and look at it,
Composing clouds and the elm
That rises opposite —
The mirror of my realm.

It takes far things and tall
And lays them at my feet
While sleepy thrushes call.
I haven't to leave my seat
To have my world complete.

1953

Sweet Death

O come sweet death, sang Bach,
Not instancing his own,
The man from Eisenach
Who kept the night alone,

Busy as it grew late
To wake the patient morn
With his own intricate
Simplicities for horn.

1950

Latter Days

Persuaded that it will be lonely later
When the lights are all out and the people gone,
I who am always an impatient waiter
Say, almost, Let the loneliness come on:
Let winter wind imprison me inside
Where no fire warms the rattling passages,
My future poor in hope, my past in pride,
With no one present but the Presences;

And let us try what loneliness entire
Will do to a mind that sometimes chose itself
Instead of company around a fire,
Or found its company along a shelf —
Let's see if I shall have the wit to bless,
Like early ills, this latter loneliness.

1953

Overseer of the Poor

The poor men's God that gives them sleep
Is not proved stingy just because
You may regard the gift as cheap.

Let them sleep sweetly on their straws
While rich men count expensive sheep.
God of the rich there never was.

1955

Goats in Pasture

Their bony heads untaxed by need of moving,
Changing, repairing, laying by,
Goats keep a comprehensive eye
On the condition of the sky —
Such store they set on keeping dry —
And live attentively, without improving.

1949

The Courthouse at Manchester

The courthouse front, both square and slender,
Is thus of that ambiguous gender
Wherein our fathers used to render
Their minds' austerity and splendor.

Within, republican yet regal,
The room surmounted by the eagle
Has seldom heard a plea inveigle
Their justice to be less than legal.

In honor to our sires who slumber,
Let us grow fit to join their number,
Who left sound forms and noble lumber
To liberate us, and encumber.

1947

On the Opening of a Superhighway

They are almost all gone who can recall
How any range of hills was once a wall,
And a hollow was a room and not a hall.

A change was a half-day's walk to the opposite range;
A wonder was a visit to the Grange
In the next hollow — strange street, new and strange.

A treat was local talent playing parts,
Dressed up and mannered so to steal our hearts,
Which seldom had the comfort of the arts.

And from these separate rooms a few went forth,
On bands of gravel winding south and north —
The few that glorified their place of birth.

1957

The Hound

Tell me about the hound
That after such a chase,
All gaunt and dusty, found
His master's strange new place

Way in the Western valley,
Threading at twilight, lame,
The maple-vaulted alley
In the village of no name —

Would I be so possessed?
Would something in me wild
Refuse to let me rest
Till I had found — my child?

1952

Under All This Slate

for Robert Francis

The bulletin of the boarding school—
Seventy lads, eleven masters—
Depicts the windowed swimming pool,
Autumnal pathways edged with asters,
Stout Georgian fronts with wide pilasters.

The Headmaster is Ph.D.
(Columbia), Princeton handles French,
English has published poetry,
The Board is winnowed from the bench,
Bar, bank, and International Wrench.

Sirs, somewhere under all this slate
You lodge, I see, a lad named Feeters.
Tell us the way he bears his fate.
Not listed with your prize competers,
Is he among your hearty eaters?

1951

All He Was Sure Of

The savage standing in the wood
Had no idea of where he stood
As to some other neighborhood.

All he was sure of, standing dumb there,
Was that he certainly stood somewhere,
And when he moved on, it was from there.

Something the same with us, only worse:
Who knows, for all our prose and verse,
Where we stand in the universe?

1959

Haying: The Comfortable Words

The farmer knee-deep on the load
Shouts, Whoa you — there, it's time you whoa'd —
You haven't got to eat every minute!
Says, This has got some green stuff in it —
We've had no weather to cure such a crop —
Well, never mind, it'll be on top.
Thundering, eh? Won't get any drier.
Don't know's I want this load much higher.
Says, Shoot, I've seen it put in wetter.
Says, This is just as good as better.

1952

Processional with Wheelbarrow

With every move I've made today
Four lambs paired up to lead the way,
Or follow, in high-tailed array.

To an unheard overture
We're marching with manure
In rites that seem obscure.

What are we out to celebrate —
The Force that makes seeds germinate,
Or the Grace that makes men meditate?

From the arch look on the features
Of four of us five creatures,
I'd say the day was Nature's.

1952

The Furniture of Earth

For all its slender girth,
The elm is stout in trouble.

The butterfly's wing power
Is masked as by a flower.

The furniture of earth
Is almost rashly noble.

1950

Something Said

Nobody's out but a winter crow
And me, of course, inspector of snow.
I almost headed back, but no:

Till something occur or be made known
I'll keep my back to the valley town
Where tomorrow's already written down.

Beyond the pasture smooth as a sheet
And the grey-green spruces capped with white
Something is being said, but what?

Something about the way a rise
Articulates with trees and skies,
Which if we knew would make us wise.

1961

Barn-Light

Barn-light on the blank snow
Assures me as I go
No time could be more proper:

Cattle are being fed,
No one has gone to bed —
I shall be home for supper.

1967

A Dream of Permanence

The house below the western wood
Already in blue shadow slept,
Though snow on the opposing slope
Still kept an amber radiance.

The time was only three o'clock,
Too early to be drawing in
To book and stove and curtains drawn
Against the icy tide of dark.

The place to stay was where I stood
Between the luster and the shade,
Not quite relinquishing the light,
Not quite yet yielding to the night,

But resting in the optic play
Whereby a house not even mine
Slept in a dream of permanence
Between an ebbing and a flood.

1958

First Day of Summer

So hushed the pupils at their play
You'd never guess this is the day
When school lets out for the whole summer.

Across the common, even dumber,
Vacationing city folk in pairs
Face newspapers in rocking chairs.

Maybe it's not for me to say —
I am a relative newcomer —
But someone ought to say hurray.

1953

Sauntering South
for Howard Frank Mosher

Sauntering south in sight
Of long blue mountains on the right,
We naturally spoke at length of letters
And the ambition of our betters —
Twain, Hawthorne, Melville, Dickinson —
To represent the many and the one,
And how their formulas
Have helped us say what is, or was,
The status of two persons of good will
Afoot at dusk on a summer hill.

1971

The Exception

One sharp old man we knew
Died doing what he loved to do,

Addressing our town meeting.
Some talked as though this might be cheating:

He should have died confined,
Out of our sight, out of his mind.

Sadly it must be said
Few men drop elegantly dead.

1963

Luck to Lovers

Let lovers all be lucky
Under the Sunday sun,
Both tongue-tied or both talky —
Their inclinations one:

To give themselves a cooling
Splash at a waterfall,
Or sun themselves while fooling
On new grass soft and small . . .

Feed them on lovers' food:
That's mutual desiring
And simultaneous mood —
And the same rate of tiring.

1966

Poor Oxford

Poor Oxford in disgrace
With fortune and men's eyes
For failing in your plays
And sonnets to disguise

Your Queen's known mind and body,
You hid your wounded name
To frustrate future study
And signed away your fame —

Vacating your estate
To make a phantom great.

1972

Numbers

We measure poems in feet
And music by the beat
To get the exact amounts
That make them just complete.
In any trade that counts
There is a life well spent
Where meaning is measurement.

1965

The Bed

Back there where we were staying,
There waiting was our bed
When we had visited
A palace or a tomb
And wanted to resume
Our interrupted playing:

There we could hardly wait
To stretch out face to face
In our own time and place
After these monuments
To stolen opulence —
Most history is hate.

1972

One Thing You Learn

One thing you learn is, most joints leak,
In pipes and porch-roofs, pockets, pens,
And people's mouths, women's and men's,
That have been trusted not to speak.

Or take a car as a case in point:
My car, perhaps a case unique,
Leaks something else from every joint.
The perfect union is yet to seek.

1957

Thistles

Oh, thistles in the field
Grow three feet tall and yield
Great thorny tubular blooms
Crowned high with purple plumes.

But these that grow in the yard
Find the going rather hard:

Thwarted by weekly mowing
To one flat leaf-set showing,
They live by playing possum—
Live without hope of blossom.

1962

Working Model

Though any hull's a thin
Shell easy to crush or rip,
To the sailor in the ship
The beautiful word is *in*.

Your smart ship model, though,
Solid from keel to rail,
Was never meant to sail,
Was only meant for show.

My model, carved with a knife,
Hollowed, and tightly decked,
Worked, and though less correct
Had room inside for life.

1962

Two Birds
(With One Stone)

I

No wonder *grackle*'s a sad word —
The grackle's a sad bird:

He hasn't any song, he squawks;
He has no hop, he flatly walks.

Ill-tempered too, he drives away
Nice birds who'd like to stay.

Unfortunate his whole design —
Nothing about him you'd call fine.

How burdensome to be a bird
For whom nobody has a good word!

II

At the opposite pole
Is the oriole

Of golden throat
And golden note

And golden name.
Is he to blame

For taking what
No grackle's got?

Why, that's your duty
If born a beauty.

1963

To Sum Up

Well may the aging poet yearn
To sum up all he's lived to learn
In a large work classical and great.

He may do better, though, to turn
Back to his small songs sharp and straight,
Loving what he loved early, late.

1950

Ring of Hills

On this high hidden farm
Are we so far from harm —
Will any ring of hills
Wall out the worldly ills?

The ring has double force:
Keeps out some ills, of course,
But any that begin
Here it keeps in.

1966

What It Took to Win

As a boy I never won a single fight.
I started some when shoved or called a sissy,
And tried to finish plenty when hit first.
I wasn't afraid of hitting or getting hit,
But never quite had what it took to win.
"Say uncle!" "Uncle," I'd say, and homeward march,
Mad all over at the rotten system
And the unbeatable, by me, world.

1964

The Blossoming Tree

Amid the lemon-greenery
Wherewith the woodland is alight,
Amid this lacy scenery
Is here and there a blossoming tree
All spicily englobed in white —
'Mid leafage no less gossamer,
The petals of a blossomer.

1952

The Things I Teach

Some nights I wake and wonder whether
The things I teach are worth the bother:

The things I know that can't be taught,
Or even said, or rightly thought —

Such as the way a keyboard phrase
Is felt to ripple as it plays,

The way our tight sonata form
Can even accommodate a storm —

Some nights I lie and wonder why
Teach, what I can teach is so dry.

1962

Mail-Time in May

Well before mail-time, on the grocery stoop
He settles, favoring one legless stub,
First of the winter-death-diminished group
Who hold their middle-of the-morning club
Outdoors in Maytime at the village hub.

Unmoved he sights along his fireless pipe
At local politics and passing fashion
A fearless eye and a mind robustly ripe
From former partisan participation —
Superior now to scorn, and to compassion.

1952

Teachers' Pay

As I walked out to smell the May,
In a darkened window on my way
A child was singing herself to sleep
With the song I taught her grade today.
Oh, teachers get nice things to keep,
To supplement their teachers' pay.

1962

High Town

Some towns of ours are so up in the air
You wonder how they hang on up there.
You almost expect the street to lurch
From your added weight on its tilted perch;
But no, it's on granite, a store and church
And six houses well out of the valleys of change —
They look across mountains, range beyond range.

1951

A Pair of Georgics

The Feed Room

The feed room on my farm
Has a fine civil charm,
With everything I use
In order ranged about:
The bins for storing feed,
Lidded against the greed
Of creatures on the loose,
The scoop to serve it out,
The feed-pans of bright tin,
The shelf for medicine
(Bag Balm and soothing talc),
The scale for measuring
The daily yield of milk
(Subtracting weight of pail),
The wall-chart with the date,
Name of the milker, weight,
The pencil on a string
Suspended from a nail,
The broom to sweep the floor,
The button-fastened door.

What civilization means
Is nothing more abstruse
Than having the right machines
At hand and fit for use.

1954

Lecture By the Professor of Pastoral Care

Let's take for an instance
My nanny named Constance,
Dear Constance my goat
(Quote Connie unquote):

She caught a hind hoof
In the slats of her stall
And raised the barn roof
With her baritone yammer
Till I came with my hammer
And pinch-bar and all,
And got her foot freed
And rubbed her sore shin
And pronounced her as fine
As she'd ever been.

But she went off her feed
And lost her bright eye,
Began to get thin
And almost went dry —
A full-fledged decline.
I couldn't think why.

She favored that foot
As though it still hurt
But I couldn't find
A thing, except dirt —
No break in the skin,
No swelling, no bruise.
It couldn't be rot.
But I bathed it and put
On an ointment I use.

And still she declined.
I finally thought,
It must be her mind —
She's afraid of that slit —
It'll catch her again.
I gave her a pen
With a solid plank floor.
By George, that was it.
She's eating once more,
Her coat is like silk,
And she's up on her milk.

A body that's nervous
Requires psychic service.

1953

Dry Noon

Their low house nooning in the maple shade,
The pair inside remember having hayed.

The day today is dry and very fine —
Good haying weather, he has said, yes sir —
He who will hay no more, come rain *or* shine.

In all the valley, not a breeze to stir
The old man's breeches drying on the line.

1957

Behind the Wall

What shall we find behind this wall,
Only the room next door?
I never went in from here before.
Better stand by in case I call —

In case when I pry off this lath
We find a sealed staircase
Or someone's secret burial place,
Or even a charmed garden path —

A pocket of old night is all.
Wait; what's this down in the dark?
A carpenter's hammer old as the ark —
The hand long dead that let you fall.

1962

Night of the South Wind

About the barefoot pair
Seen striding with blown hair
Into their secret place
In the dark behind the school:

Let's say they strip and chase
Each other, snapping belts,
Then dressed pad somewhere else
To eat before they cool
Themselves in someone's pool
Or in the gathering shower
That'll break within the hour;

All night this is their town
To prowl in up and down,
To sport and laugh and leap
While the old owners sleep.

1972

Evening Prayer

Would anybody come
If Evening Prayer were said?
Priest, choir, all Christendom
Apparently are dead

Who here in afterglow
Sang-in the summer night,
And often through dense snow
Trudged here to pray for light.

1975

Hymn 306

Had I become a priest
Seldom would I have ceased
From praying or at least

Kneeling
Under some holy ceiling . . .

As it is, I seldom rest
From writing hymns you hadn't guessed
Were hymns, the way they're dressed.

1978

Between the Rails

The flower between the rails
Where downbound freight trains roll
Lives inches from disaster
In turbulence and quakes:
Inches are all it takes.

1980

My Instruments

Twelve stops and seven ranks —
Organ was once my wonder:
My pedals and key-banks
Performed orchestral jobs
And spoke with a lush thunder
When I drew all the knobs.

Piano soon came back
As my first instrument:
Whatever it might lack
In blast and simulation
It freed me to invent.
Thank God for limitation.

1966

The Cold Hotel

A closet door stood at the window pane
As late sun streaked the mountainside through rain —
The summer gone would never come again.

The mountain, though, would stay the winter through,
Even with no one to admire the view
While waiting for the dinner gong.

And both were real — the hollow cold hotel
So lonely present, and the absent throng
It could not call again from where they dwell.

1951

Anniversary Posy

Shopping the whole fair through
For something nice for you
At, say, a dollar or two,
I found the poet's booth
Handles the cheapest truth:
How will this posy do,
In memory of our youth?

1951

Nothing to Do

Still day, late fall;
Low cloud encloses all,
Gray ceiling and gray wall.
The sawmill's whine is muffled.

No wind comes sporting by;
There are no leaves on high
To rush if they were ruffled.

Her last defenses down,
Earth has no business of her own
But waits the pleasure of the sky.

Nothing to do but wait and see
If rain it be
In a chilly douse,

Or snow, the season's first
At midnight when we aren't around
Gaining upon the ground
Where summer lies dispersed —

Soon we shall waken in a snow-lit house.

1949

Prelude To

Still the worst blasphemy that we commit
Is treating any time as prelude to:

Day as the time before we close and quit,
Night as the time before we rise and do.

Be out in loving care till day goes west;
Then in, to inward love of dark and rest.

1957

Book Review

Has he developed as a writer —
Grown better as his hair grew whiter?

Not really, early work aside;
He's stayed much the same since he hit his stride.

But knowing what age can do to verse,
Let's praise him for not growing worse.

1969

What a Poem Is

A poem is what you do about a fact —
A poem is an act.

A poem is what the mind does at its best —
Is an intelligence test.

A poem is a performance — on a stage
No larger than a page.

1957

Permanent Surprise

A *permanent* surprise?
Yes, what a poem supplies:

Unlike most jokes and stunts
Which seldom work but once,

The coil-springs of fine rhyme
Go off — ping — every time

Because it's not just wit,
Though wit is part of it;

The rest of it is heart,
The everlasting part.

1978

Mason's Trick

From masons laying up brick
To build a rosy wall
Level and square and tall,

We borrow a mason's trick,
Or at least a builder's term:
Rhymes keep our corners firm.

1967

Testifying

Why, if the world is dying,
Why must I, crying,
Keep testifying?

My sense that all is lost
Can't quite defeat my trust
That all will last.

1971

Under the Holy Eye

The world and I when young
And backward and content
Were visible among
The several bodies hung
About the firmament

Under the holy eye.
Though we all strove alone,
Some cloistered behind stone,
Some under the wide sky,
Our struggles yet were known,

Our Bibles still were true.
Then everything proved vast,
And numerous, and fast,
And, Father, either you
Or we flew out of view.

1959

The Wet and the Dark

This rain's no inconvenience to the beaver,
But makes tame cattle huddle at the gate;
I too have been as much at home in the river
As in this thin air where we stand and wait.

This dark's no disadvantage to the cat,
But makes tame people huddle by the fire;
I too've gone prowling through the liquid black
In company with old sweet damned desire.

1961

Sun in Winter

More welcome in the house in these short days
Than at any other season is the sun,
Who yellows now the walls of our south rooms
And gilds the bubbles of steam-beaded bowls
On kitchen tables, while outdoors the eaves
Slow raining sunlit drops, and down the track
An engine idling, warm the winter noon.

1936

Love of Snow

In those years, days like this
When storm made the oak leaves hiss
Were days of winter bliss:

Pulling our sleds to the top
Of town where houses stop
And fields and pastures drop

Over back to farms and the river,
We'd slide and climb forever —
Till first dark made us shiver;

Then homeward tired and slow,
Ready for kitchen glow,
All white from love of snow.

1950

Time to Plant Trees

Time to plant trees is when you're young
So you will have them to walk among —

So, aging, you can walk in shade
That you and time together made.

1970

Going a Long Journey
for Eunice Young Craig

I know what things to pack,
But what to leave to you
In case I don't come back —
And then, what if I do?
I wish one of us knew.

This life is done the day
I lock that door and go:
Till then we have to play
We don't know what we know —
And know what we don't know.

1976

The Polypody

The idea of the Gothic vault
Is in the polypody fern
Which springs from a clustered base
In flaring arcs
With vertical and transverse ribs.

When the Gothic builders set about
Paving the steep
Highdrive to Heaven with curved
And fitted stone, their first blueprint
Was this green pattern in the woods.

1964

Belfry

for Garret Keizer

A town should have a tower
And on the tower a clock
And in the tower a bell
Chiming each quarter-hour
To notify the flock
That everything is well,

Especially at night
When somebody seems bound
To suffer dislocation;
That's when a handmade height
Letting down quiet sound
Can uphold civilization.

1975

Old Fellow

Mouth open, the old fellow sleeps in the sun
On the tired bench that spans the polished granite
Corner of the monument in the city park.
If the bench should give way, he'd be cut in two . . .
What bothers us most about him, though, in passing,
Is the idea that he's not well connected:
Homeless, no doubt, and churchless, collegeless —
It may be even lawless — can it be
He's so far gone as to care nothing for
All that these institutions codify?
To think of anyone letting the future come
Upon him as it wills, unfiltered through
The bronze grille of the First National Bank!

1942

High Meadow

Tonight in the high meadow they're still haying
In the perfect weather for which they've been praying.

With truck and tractor headlights on high beam
Making the landscape unreal as a dream,

They're getting in a well-cured bumper crop;
When haying's this good, no one wants to stop.

1969

Two Basic Facts

I

Poets are who is glad
When anyone is having
The best time to be had.

II

The saddest fact I know
Is that tranquility
Is neglect of others' woe.

1967 and 1950

Idle Hound

As an idle hound busily lopes all over,
Through fences, up a field, across a yard,
Along the highway home, with springy gait,
Tail swinging, ears a-flop: so I as lover
Of this terrain and people, local bard,
Busily saunter round and speculate.

1950

Summer Is Swift

Summer is swift and turns not back.
Sequence of berries is straw, rasp, blue, and black;
Of minor field-life, hyla, firefly, locust.
In each a two-weeks age is focused.

1952

My Inch

You who will come to judge me
I pray may not begrudge me
My inch upon your shelves,
But yield me, as yourselves
Aspire to be served,
This point at which I stand
As on a spectral band
In high heaven hugely curved,
Point after infinite point
To infinite rays conjoint,
Each ray a street to enter
The world and tap its center,
Each point a frail distinction
Against time and extinction.

1949

Delivering a Poem

You slip in past his guard,
Hit him exactly square
And adequately hard,
And get right out of there.

1951

Light

Be light on your feet:
Your prints exact
Step evenly from fact to fact —
Be light, be neat.

Let light in your eyes:
Look where the sun cures hay.
Like water under open day
Be clear — grow wise.

Light fire to greet
All whom bad weather
Brings in to hope awhile together —
Give light, give heat.

1946

The Same Old Drive

Cause of the coming war
Will be the same old drive
That saved the race before:
The oldest drive we've had
Kept us alive
And let us thrive
But also made us bad.

1967

A Beaten Man

Defy your father and defeat him;
He can't very well fight back
Except by counter-attack —
He'd rather let you beat him.

However, once you've disobeyed him,
You may not relish what you've made him.

1987

For John Frederic Moore
Amherst College 1933

What of the selfless case
Of one who leaves no trace
But his unselfish acts?

How to discern his face,
And how prolong his grace,
From such mute artifacts?

1950

Always Free

Squirrels are always free
To leap from tree to tree
And every time connect,

Or any time descend
A trunk headfirst and end
This death-defying act.

1986

Two Squirts

"In the eyes of a man of imagination,
Nature is imagination itself." —William Blake

The Skunk

You talk about imagination — think:
A creature armed with nothing but a stink
Propelled to make aggressors stop and blink.

About his bad name as a dirty fighter,
Compared, say, to a scratcher or a biter,
You have to ask what makes it so much righter

To kill an enemy than make him cough
Just long enough so you can get clean off.

The Squid

The squid, more like the skunk than you might think,
Considering his home is in the drink,
Confounds his enemies by squirting ink.

About *his* ill fame as a dirty fighter,
Compared, say, to a Congressman or writer,
You have to ask why it's so much politer

To ruin an enemy than make him blink
Just long enough so you can rise or sink.

1964

After the Recital

What waits the artist after the recital,
A solo coffee in a night café?

As if anything but love could feed the vital
Hunger of one come home from worlds away.

1955

Each Other

They'd no idea what use
They might be to each other,

She still in her late youth,
He older than her father;

It seemed they had been left
Each other as a gift.

1983

The Cost of Being What I Am

The cost of being what I am is high
In comfortable certainties foregone:
I cannot say for certain that the sky
Is Heaven, nor that a bearded God looks on;

I cannot claim the damages I cause
Are justified by my unworldly ways,
Though I am surer than I ever was
That what I celebrate deserves my praise.

When you, aloft, my namesake and my son,
Attempt the balances that are my art,
I see my penitence has just begun
For having failed to teach you safer sport.

I didn't know the bargain that I made
Would bring this heavy reckoning to be paid.

1954

The Boss's Dog

When the boss's dog attacked my son
I got kind words from everyone.

But when the moment came to act
You'd be surprised how they backtracked:

The minister couldn't get too sore
At such a large contributor,

Nor did the aldermen and mayor
Want to offend the chief taxpayer.

As for the workmen in his shop,
What would they do if that should stop?

And soon the butcher and the baker
Were calling me a trouble-maker:

He was a longtime resident
And I an upstart malcontent —

Until to hear the dialog
You'd think my son attacked the dog.

1973

A Profitable Dealing

Some days the heart would fail
From future-fright and loathing
Did not the belly frail
With need of food and clothing

Compel us to maintain
A profitable dealing
With partners of our pain,
Whose patience is our healing.

1951

Egg in the Pocket

Go pocket a fresh egg
And then go bump that leg
Next time you come to turn

A corner in the barn;

Maybe someday you'll learn
What not to leave to chance —
Including nice dry pants.

1950

Choirmaster

Hearing the sweet birds take the sky
On sunny waves of lilac scent,
As local choirmaster I
Would have us follow where they went
And, like them, toss our notes so high
We feel and cause astonishment.

1982

Egress

A poem should have an ending
As a device for sending
Its readers back to tending
Their mowing or their mending

Free as may be from doubt
Of what it was about —
And in no need to shout
For help in getting out.

1951

Light-Minded Dame
Evelyn S. Lease 1866–1957

Come in. Give me a minute and I'll name you—
Of course—how are you, James? It's been some years.
Don't be alarmed—my mind is pretty good;
It's slow, that's all—it likes to take its time.
You're getting bald, too, aren't you? Never mind.
Why are we so surprised when young friends age?
Well now, you'll eat a piece of gingerbread?
I made myself some gingerbread and cream,
Just for a treat. The appetite's one sense
That doesn't fail. I heard Dr. Eliot—
You know, forever President of Harvard—
At a librarians' convention tell
Of calling on an aged dame who might,
He hoped, be led to say a weighty thing
About the meaning of life. He asked her what
As she looked back had meant the most to her.
"My vittles," she replied. Second the motion.
Here. Oh, you'll want a spoon. So 'tis you find me,
Devising treats and wasting time I ought
To spend on cramming for my finals—ha!
(You know: Why's Grandma always reading her Bible?
Well, son, I guess she's cramming for her finals.)
But come—look here—the funeral home, remember?
As a rule I see it from this back window.
See there, it's almost hidden by the snowbank.
That must account for my light-mindedness.

1952

Why She Stayed

Toward noon he spoke of it again: "Daughter,
Why don't you go — why don't you marry him?"

The two of them were cutting pulp in the swamp
At the far end of the farm. The sun was hot;
Despite the flies, they'd shed the woolen shirts
They wore coming out in the misty morning.

For answer, she impatiently shook her head.

Slowly he straightened up, laid down his ax,
Glanced at the sun. "You ready for your dinner?"

Again she shook her head, bending more deeply
Over the new-felled cedar she was trimming.

"You want to work a while more?"

                                 "I can't eat."

"You mustn't work without eating. Want to go home?"

"No, I'm all right."

                       "You may get hungry later.
Let's work a while more." He picked up his ax,
Then laid it down again. "Cassie," he said,
"I don't intend to boss. You'll do as you like.
I'm puzzled, that's all. Why don't you want to go?
Why don't you want to marry?"

                              "I don't know."

"Don't you like Charley Burgess?"

                         "Yes — "

                         "Then why — "

"I want to stay with you."

                 "Why, bless your heart.
I'm glad to have you — you know that."

                          "I'll stay."

"But Cassie, look, there's other things to think of.
Don't you want your own home? Don't you want children?"

"Isn't this my own home?"

                              "And I'm your child?
In a way, I am. You have looked after me
Since you were twelve and Mother died of the flu.
You've done a woman's work since you were twelve."

"This isn't woman's work!" With a flourish she
Clipped off the final branch.

                              "No, and I hate —"

"I like it! Don't you see, Pa? Charley doesn't.
He thinks you abuse me. He won't say so, but
That's what he thinks."

                    "Charley thinks that?"

                                        "Yes, Pa.
He says he won't have me out in the woods,
Or even in the barn. That's what he says.
A woman's work, he says, is in the house —
Dishes and cooking, sewing, making beds —"

"Well, Charley's right, of course."

                              "Oh Pa!"

                                        "In the main.
If it wasn't for my wounded knee —"

                                   "That's it,
That's it — you need me, see? That's the whole point."

"No, daughter, that is not the point. The point
Is you, not me. What future is there for you
In nursing me along for a few years?
You won't have any clothes — look at you, dressed
In old patched pants and shirt like — well, like me!

You won't have a nice house with electric lights,
You won't have any fun — "

                              "I'll make us bowls
Of popcorn over the kitchen fire at night,
Now won't I, Pa?"

                    "Yes, Cassie, I'm sure you will."

"All right. Now where'd you put the lunch? Oh, here.
What do you want first, egg or tomato sandwich?"

"Egg. I'm not hungry now. Cassie, I wonder — "

"What do you wonder, Pa?"

                              "You've had so little,
I wonder if you don't mistrust good luck."

"Why Pa, my luck is wonderful! Here, eat."

So Cassie stayed and did her woman's work,
And turned into the toothless, furtive creature
Occasional visitors to her crippled father
Spy peeking through the doorway-crack today.

And so the folks down in the village say,
"He worked the poor girl till she lost her mind."

1953

A Gift
for you

Sure, you could call it cheap,
Or you could call it thrift,
This poem I make a gift
Of and still get to keep.

1970

Will You Be Here?

She'd run off with him to a shack in the woods
In winter—one tar-paper-covered room,
One window and a door, a stove, a bed.
Folks in the village couldn't understand
Why in the world she'd left her upstairs rent
With new linoleums, white sink, oil range,
For such a life as this. The man she'd left,
Her husband, was a quiet, steady sort,
Son to the man who owned the lumber mill,
And would no doubt own it someday himself;
This other, a boy still wet behind the ears,
Still talking big of what he meant to do.

The husband took it to the minister
For help. They drove in to the end of the logging road,
Then waded in to the shack through knee-deep snow.
"Good Lord!" the husband said, "Good Lord Almighty!"
The tin-pipe chimney sent a little smoke
Into the hemlock boughs. The pair were at home.
The minister said they'd like to talk with her—
Alone. The boy, leaving, paused and turned
To her: "Will you be here when I come back?"

1937

A Body In the Fog
Warren W. Hartwell 1869–1956

I drove my hearse—that is, I call it a hearse—
A panel truck is what it really is—
I drove from Barton over to Westmore village,
And Albert Gates met me right there by the church
With a pung sleigh to drive up and fetch the body.
Middle of the winter, but there'd been a thaw,
Mild, with some rain—the snow in the road was soft.
You know that road up the hill there by the church-steep.
I noticed, going up, every time the horse

144

Leaned into it pretty good, Albert pulled back
Hard on the reins to ease him into his collar.
"I dunno," he said, "whether this harness'll stand it.
I patched 'er best I could before I come.
Some odds and ends I had around the barn.
Maybe she'll hold together, maybe she won't."
"Well, we got up there all right, and Freeman and I —
I'd brought Freeman along to help — we got
Little Jimmy into my basket and onto the pung.
He was a little Irishman was Jimmy,
Took sick about noon and died in a couple hours.
They sent for me to do him up. He'd come
To this country when he was about fifteen
And settled later in Westmore on that farm,
Nice farm. They guessed his age at eighty-five.
We got him loaded in and started back down.
Well sir, the first little water-bar we came to,
The horse gave a heave and walked right out of his harness.
"There," Albert said. "I'll have to go down to the Gove place
And see what I can borrow for harness gear."
"You take your horse along," I says, "and fix
The whole concern at once and bring him back."
So off he went. By now 'twas really dark,
And foggy, say! That floating, flapping stuff
That sails around in scuds in a thawing spell.
And there we were, stuck off on that hill with a body.
"He'll be an hour," I said to Freeman, "at least.
Let's see if you and I can't free this pung."
We'd nosed smack into a bank of snow. You know
How Freeman's built — there ain't a wider man
In the whole state of Vermont. I told him, "Freeman,
You get between the thills" — he filled 'em, too.
I got behind and pulled careful on the basket
And we backed her up a little and got her loose.
Off we went down the hill with Freeman drawing.
I tell you it was a gloomy night to be out in,

With all that creeping fog, even with no body.
We hadn't gone very far when we commenced
To see flashes of dancing light all round,
In with these scuds of fog. My hair rose up,
And so did Freeman's. We stopped and got closer together.
"It's Jimmy," I whispered, "it's Jimmy doing that."
I thought his soul might not care much for the way
We were handling his body — or something might not care —
He was an Irishman . . . After a minute
I said, "Let's get him out of here," and we
Went back to moving the sleigh, holding our breath.
Well, we got down to Gove's — you know what it was?
Albert was out in the yard there at the Gove place
Working on the harness with a lantern
That had a hole in the chimney big as this cup.
That lamp-flame was a-flickering all over,
And being reflected off those scuds of fog.
He got the harness mended and we hitched up.
Gove offered to let us take the lantern. "No,"
I said. "You keep the miserable guttering thing.
We'll be a good deal better off in the dark."

1952

My Voice

My voice, you are more honest than my hand:
I scarce can make you utter an untruth
Except those white deceptions not uncouth
That you perform at charity's command.
You'd leave me not one false or cruel tooth.
Whereas this hand — is it perennial youth
Or settled viciousness makes it so bland
A tool of words too clever or too grand?

My hand has scribbled that my heart is broken,
My hand has scribbled that I am alone —
Such solemn nonsense you have never spoken.
The breath by you intaken and outspent,
Flowing from firmament to firmament,
Has made the true stars neighbor to my bone.

1951

Composing

Composing too, I would have been a debtor
To history: I could only compose
In the old alphabet our culture knows
Where are we like to find an alphabetter?

Though some claim Beethoven exhausted it
By saying all that it could say,
Brahms and Tchaikovsky found it adequate.
Not that they said what we would say today —

If only our generation didn't feel
Compelled to re-invent the wheel.

1967

Six Bits

1. ACHIEVEMENT
You either achieve what you believe
Or else believe what you achieve.

1950

2. FRESHMAN
Freshman is one who looks to someone slicker
For proper attitudes to God and liquor.

1950

3. CONTEMPT BREEDS ENVY
The danger of despising what you haven't got
Is that you'll come to have it, like as not.

1954

4. MERRY
Lord, make us merry —
A little if not very.

1956

5. CAIRNS
What use are all these cairns we raise to mark
Our little one-way journey through the dark?

1964

6. THE GREAT PAIR
Dr. Johnson was not a great writer, but Boswell was;
Boswell was not a great man, but Johnson was.

1988

The Great Question

The question is the thing;
All answers are opinion.

So don't risk answering —
Not even a suggestion —
Just frame the quiz.

And the great question is
What *is* the question?

1954

Our Situation

What would be worse
Would be an ill-run universe.

This one's run well
As near as we can tell,

Been running a good while
In satisfactory style,

And seems prepared to run
Until it thinks it's done —

Still young and giving birth
After the death of Earth,

Still bright as first begun
Beyond the loss of Sun —

We ought to be elated
To be so situated.

1990

Useful Men

Praise useful men
Withstanding cold or heat
In open field or stuffy pen
Breeding a rust free wheat
Or buxom hen
To give the world more food:
Bless any citizen
Who feeds the multitude.

1974

A Second Pair of Georgics

The Avenger of Injustice

That day the old buck rammed
The little kid
That could barely keep its feet
And stretched it bleating on the ground,
I blew my lid.
I damned
Him and I beat
Him with my fists.
I am so sick of seeing folks pushed around,
So seldom in position to enter the lists.
If I had had a gun
The census on my place would have read less one.

He stood right still, the gentle brute,
And let me pound.
He looked surprised,
But his hide is tough.
When I had had enough —
My hands are sore —
I wondered why I'd been so exercised.
I found the kid
Who'd tottered off and hid,
Not hurt, just scared,
And told it someone cared.
I may have given it a kiss.
And then I patted the buck:
Go thou and butt no more.
If I had had the terrible luck
To kill him, would that have evened any score?
I seldom do a thing like this.

1953

In Capricorn, On Asphodel

The goat too sick to keep
The vet consigned to sleep.
"Good-by," I said, "goodby.
My fault you had to die.
Good browsing in the sky.
This afternoon dine well
In Capricorn, on asphodel."

"Oh, never mind her soul!
You say you've dug a hole?"
I had prepared her grave.
She was too sick to save.

I unbuckled her collar.
"Leave it. We'll use it to haul 'er."
He hauled her, and dropped her in.
Gentler I should have been,
And yet he wasn't ungentle,
Just brisk, unsentimental,
Wasting no time on a goner.
We shoveled the dirt in on her.

1953

Appearances

On houses that I pass
I like to guess which glass
They mostly look out through —
Which panes give them their view
Of what goes on out here —
Where you and I appear.

1989

Builder's Hands

Houses you've helped to build,
By whomsoever filled,
Are yours
As much as theirs:
The floors
That hold their chairs
The passageways and doors
That pattern their affairs,
Also the stairs
They climb to sleep or love,
Being knit with nails you drove —
Their entire building stands
By virtue of your hands.

1953

My Living Room

My living room's just right
For length and breadth and height
And privacy with light.

Its broad bay-window niche
With neat serrated arch
Would trim a little church.

Sure, famous rooms are older,
Bigger, and mostly colder.
Mine's in no travel folder,

But who has living space
Of greater use or grace?
Beauty can show its face

Under an ancient dome
In Paris or in Rome,
Or in a country home.

1959

No Exile

Why don't she go away —
Unwed and big with child?
But she, self-reconciled,
Ignored this. No, I'll stay

Among my kind, my folks;
Who in the world should know
Better how to forego
The unkindest of jokes?

A few continued shocked,
Daughter to one of whom
Shortly required a groom,
Who hastily was booked.

The tranquil one meanwhile
Remained and bore her son,
Fathered by everyone,
And friended — no exile.

And she always each day
Accepts her sentence new
As all of us must do
Whose fault gives us away.

1950

At a Grave

You were a modern prince, a born possessor —
Strength, looks, and brains, the title of professor —
Third anyway in a distinguished line:
I used to wish that what you had were mine.

You did not have to live on hopes and shadows,
Nor have to count on dying without honors.
Yet here we are, you in the grave you chose,
And I still bearing tolerable woes.

1962

The Act

Back up and let's foresee
The act that will plant me
In my mother's womb:

May she and he
In a pleasant room
Have tender unity.

1991

Everybody Goes

If my surmise is right,
Birds look ahead
To their autumnal flight
With neither joy nor dread:

All anybody knows
Is everybody goes.

1991

Wet Socks

Nothing I own
Is sure to improve with time
Like these wet socks
On the radiator
That I'll put on
Dry and warm
Later.

1971

School's Out

For perfect pleasure here's my entry:
Driving at ease in pleasant country
(The engine doing all the work),

Starting a summer-long vacation
From a demanding occupation,
Looking at Willoughby and Burke.

1956

Afterword   Something Seen and Told

Amid their rich displays of knit
Or woven goods, enameled ware,
Stained glass, wood carving, pottery,
The proud embarrassed craftsmen sit
And look as if they didn't care
Whether we're sold on what we see.

At craft shows held in northeastern Vermont throughout the year, one proud and not-so-embarrassed craftsman is a septuagenarian poet handing out free samples of his work. "Would you like a poem?" he asks with the unaffectedness of a train conductor.

Those who've been to the shows before know him by sight, perhaps by name. He is James Hayford, "the poet." They may have last year's poem hung behind a refrigerator magnet, or they may have a copy of his recent novel for children, *Gridley Firing*.

Those acquainted with Hayford or with odd bits of literary history know him as the one who received "the laying on of hands" from Robert Frost, the one whom contemporary poet X. J. Kennedy has called the "unofficial New England poet laureate." To close friends, he is even more.

"I think he's the wisest person I've ever met," said the novelist Howard Frank Mosher. "Jim is a great man in the way you'd want your president to be . . . I can remember where I was sitting when I met Jim Hayford for the first time just the way people remember where they were and what they were doing when Kennedy was shot. That's how important this was to me."

I can remember where I was, too. I was at a craft show. And before I even read my free poem, I sensed that the man handing it to me had come to his little booth by a journey stubbornly his own. I could sense that it would make sense to hear him say:

No one likes feeling weak
Or looking so antique,

But I love being old
With something seen and told.

I'd have never guessed, though, how much there was to tell.

The road that brought Hayford to the craft show and the Northeast Kingdom and his own distinct place on our bookshelves is one best described in his own words. A good beginning is his poem "The Waves," which he affixed as an epigraph to an early volume of verse, *Processional with Wheelbarrow* (1970):

The green waves mount, crash coolly, turn, and run.
Their glints are old and new under the sun.
The timeless and the temporary are one.

In the emptiness of their uneasy pause
I hear myself recollecting who I was—
Identity, my papers, my lost cause.

Talking to Hayford about his life, one is audience to a recollection of "causes," some lost, and others hard won.

The first of these was poetry itself. In 1935, having asked the president of Amherst College for the funds to do so, Robert Frost awarded the first and only Robert Frost Fellowship. The recipient was enjoined to stay away from art colonies, graduate schools, big cities, and Europe—in short, to be "saved" for American poetry from what Frost viewed as its cankers—and to produce a work within 20 years. Frost awarded his fellowship to "the boy I thought most capable of making up his mind."

More than 50 years later Hayford still wonders why he should have been that boy. "I'm not known for making up my mind," he says. "I never was. This is one of the mysteries—how did Frost get that impression?"

Perhaps he got it from the poem Hayford recited as his college's "Ivy Poet," in which a young man chooses poetry over music as his life's work. Or, he may have taken his impression from an earlier "cause." Hayford resigned from his college fraternity after a student was denied membership when it was learned he was Jewish. He can still remember a professor's wife shaking her umbrella at him as he walked across campus and shrieking, "You traitor! You miserable traitor! "

The Frost Fellowship proved to be a sobering graduation prize. "I knew that encouragement by Frost was good for five minutes' euphoria and then you came thumping down to say 'Well, what do I do about all of this?' " After marrying his first cousin, Helen Emerson, Hayford began his lifelong rhythm of writing, teaching, music lessons, and manual labor, often accompanied by the penury of each. In the 1930s he helped found Goddard College, which he still sees as "a progressive attempt to remedy the deficiencies of standard institutions."

The most political of Hayford's causes occurred in 1948, when he joined the presidential campaign of Progressive Party candidate Henry Wallace. The Progressives called for nuclear rapprochement with the Russians. Since the Communist Party ran no candidate of its own that year, choosing instead to endorse Wallace, Hayford's commitment did little to recommend him to the southern Vermont community where he was then teaching school. In the face of growing controversy, he resigned his position.

If the episode had ended there, it might have been a simple case of two roads that diverged, Hayford having taken "the one less traveled by." But Hayford was to diverge even from his fellow travelers. Disturbed by what he saw as a decidedly anti-United States tone in the party platform, he and a friend authored what came to be known as "the Vermont Resolution," which would have put the Progressives on record as not giving blanket approval to the foreign policy of any nation. Hayford introduced the resolution on the floor of the national convention in Philadelphia. H. L. Mencken gave a slightly biased firsthand account: "When an honest but humorless Yankee from Vermont tried to get in a plank disclaiming any intention to support the Russian assassins in every eventuality, no matter how outrageous their doings, it was first given a hard parliamentary squeeze by the Moscow fuglemen on the platform, and then bawled to death on the floor."

Friends of Hayford will find more than a little ironic humor in "humorless Yankee." There is also irony and, at a distance, some humor in what followed. A communist from outside Vermont phoned Hayford and asked him how much the capitalists had bribed him to split the convention. Meanwhile the Communist Party in Vermont, the whole handful, invited Hayford to join. He politely declined. With the local press clamoring for him to "go back to Russia," he moved with Helen and their young son to West Burke to raise goats, conduct a church choir—and write more poetry.

It was in West Burke that Hayford first heard his own voice clearly speaking in his poems. Until that time he had struggled to achieve his own persona against the background of Frost's influence. "It's a great blessing to have a great man get interested in you. But it also constitutes a work, a task, to find yourself under that enormous shadow." The task, he says, "doesn't make you a great man; it doesn't make you a great poet. It doesn't make you anything but yourself."

When Hayford took his new work to Frost, the elder poet also acknowledged the new voice. "Now, I wouldn't say what you say here," he began, "but I'm forgetting your way is different from mine." That was what Hayford had hoped to hear.

In what may be his own favorite poem, we can hear Hayford's voice, and perhaps the clearest statement of his philosophy.

To Learn to Swim

Let the child learn to swim
Where it's too deep for him
To touch his toes to sand:
Let him right then begin

To *be* in when he's in
By doing without land.

Let him for his own sake
Require himself to make
It from the end of the dock
Out to the diving float,
Or further out, to a boat
Or some deep-water rock—

Keeping his head and breath
While buoyed by certain death.

Hayford has often required himself "to make / It from the end of the dock" to some place "Where it's too deep." "And still . . . I like to swim where I can touch my toes to sand. l haven't ever gotten over the flubbing stage and I never will, of course. . . . But my life has been spent in the attempt to organize the flubbing, to organize my attitude towards the flubbing. . . . My philosophy of flubbing has gotten refined over the years to the point where I forget I've flubbed!" And here the humorless Yankee's eyes twinkle. "This is what comes of higher speculation."

In the decades when Hayford was working to establish his own poetic voice, he was also moving away from the mainstream of contemporary American poetry. Or, rather, it was moving away from him. Like Frost and Emily Dickinson, Hayford is a formalist, one who writes in meter and rhyme.

From masons laying up brick
To build a rosy wall
Level and square and tall,

We borrow a mason's trick,
Or at least a builder's term:
Rhymes keep our corners firm.

The subject, shape, and simplicity of a poem like "Mason's Trick" all seemed old-fashioned at a time when most established poets wrote in free verse, and many others inclined toward academic obscurity. His first appearances in *Harper's* and *The New Yorker* were followed by a long period in which the only one who seemed willing to publish Hayford was Hayford himself.

Now with the publication of *Star in the Shed Window: Collected Poems 1933–1988* (Shelburne: New England Press, 1989) Hayford may, at age 75, be coming to the attention he deserves, to what Auden called

> A poet's hope: to be,
> like some valley cheese,
> local, but prized elsewhere.

Still, one wonders how many "prized" poets would not envy a man whose verses neighbors carry in their coat pockets like good luck charms or hang up in their kitchens. "They wouldn't do this, I don't think," Hayford says, "just because it's me—because I'm not Robert Frost, I'm not anybody to be paid attention to except as I say something."

Anyone who reads the *Collected Poems* will agree: Hayford does say something, and he is not Robert Frost or an imitation of Robert Frost. Howard Frank Mosher notes, among other differences between the two poets, Hayford's concern with the small towns in which he has lived most of his life. "His world is closer to Jane Austen's world than it is to Robert Frost's. . . . It's the world of Montpelier—which wasn't much more than a village, really, when Jim was growing up there—of West Burke, of Orleans."

We see Hayford's world in poems like these:

January Night

> The shiny trodden snow
> In harsh illumination,
> So cold your bootsoles creak;
> The houses double-glassed
> Against the searching blast—
> These things you may have classed
> Under the heading, Bleak.

Fact is, the snow was trod
By people warmly shod
And coated—none in mink—
Sashaying to and fro
Betwixt the stores, the station,
Tavern, and house of God,
And this bright, crowded rink.

Two Old Gents

Two old gents standing nose to nose
Are generally engaged in talk;
I see with something of a shock
These are about to come to blows.

It may be they won't hurt each other,
It would hurt me to watch them tussle.
Youth is the time for a show of muscle—
Which may be stopped by someone's mother.

We also see in a number of poems what Mosher points to as Hayford's deepest conviction—that people have to get along in a difficult world. This idea forms the basis of Hayford's children's novel, *Gridley Firing*, in which a skunk named after C. V. Gridley, captain of the flagship of Vermont's Admiral George Dewey, teaches a young farm boy the relationship between self-defense and self-control. Hayford also celebrates the skunk's "gentle" deterrence in a poem:

You talk about imagination—think:
A creature armed with nothing but a stink
Propelled to make aggressors stop and blink .

About his bad name as a dirty fighter,
Compared, say, to a scratcher or a biter,
You have to ask what makes it so much righter

To kill an enemy than make him cough
Just long enough so you can get clean off.

What impresses one most of all, in the poems and in Hayford's own conversation about poetry, is his sense of highest obligation to the reader. It is important to Hayford that his reader understand, enjoy, find value—above all, that he or she be "played fair" with. Otherwise, in his view, "the reader quite rightly says 'I trusted this man and he betrayed me. He has not lived up to his share of the bargain.'"

Perhaps this is part of what makes Hayford a Vermont poet—assuming we care more than he does about defining such things. It is the sense that while other people matter not at all as dictators of one's life, they matter a great deal as beneficiaries of one's work. It is the attitude that says no one had better tell me what kind of cows to raise or verse to write, but I insist on providing good milk or a readable poem. And I refuse to uphold either value without the other.

A boy in an Orleans restaurant was overheard describing his music teacher. "Mr. Hayford walks, and he walks, and he thinks!" Now retired from school-teaching, Hayford is still a recognizable sight as he walks daily through this small mill town. There is no art colony here, no college— no trace of Europe but in its name. The conditions of the Frost Fellowship have been carried out well beyond their intent.

James and Helen Hayford have lived in Orleans for 34 of their 52 married years. He once lost a teaching job in this town for helping lead the fight for a uniform salary schedule within the school district. But when he retired from his last teaching post at Winooski High School, he returned to Orleans. Here he spends much of his time revising old poems, writing new ones, working on his novel *Shakespeare's Ghost* (based on the "crackpot" theory that Shakespeare's plays and sonnets are in fact the work of the Earl of Oxford), reading eclectically and robustly, maintaining what amounts to a wayside kitchen-shrine for aspiring or disgruntled writers, artists, and other lost souls, and sharing in the modest cultural life of a small community.

"I can't imagine any other contemporary poet I know," says Howard Frank Mosher, "going down and working with the choir on Thursday night and then on Friday morning going in and talking to the third graders and then on Saturday spending all day editing a book for the local historical society." X. J. Kennedy has written: "I don't know another poet whose life and work make such a seamless whole."

One wonders, though, how Hayford reckons his own life as he walks through town, how he sees the success that has come, he notes, "just about in time."

Lately he has begun to receive fan letters. He has had a handful of interviews, a radio appearance, a college lecture, a banquet. "What a shame it couldn't have happened earlier," he told Helen. "We could have been eager to go. Now I wonder, am I going to make it?"

By the drugstore that sells *Gridley Firing* and *At Large on the Land* next to the *Farmer's Almanac* and *Good Housekeeping*, Hayford turns the corner, crosses the railroad tracks, and climbs North Avenue past Dee Dee's Daycare to his house on a hill above the furniture factory.

> Out of the money which
> Causes the rich,
>
> I stay friends with the poor
> Whom I write for.

For some, James Hayford has finally "made it" with the collection and publication of his poems. For others, the poet "arrived" when he first set foot in Orleans, or when he set up his first booth at a craft fair—whenever he came to accept his task as that of forming useful words for ordinary people in the midst of a difficult world. "I suppose the hope in general of all the operations I've undertaken in my lifetime is that I can contribute some clarity to the chaos that goes on around us, which is the hope of everybody who weaves a blanket or shapes a pot."

To those of us who hang his verses in our kitchens, who glance at them on the way to work or in the rush to cook supper, it is a hope fulfilled every day.

GARRET KEIZER

[The above article first appeared in the Winter 1989 issue of *Vermont Life*, under the title "Yankee Rebel," with photographs by Owen Stayner. In the spring of 1993 Jim was awarded an honorary degree of Doctor of Humane Letters by the University of Vermont. Jim died June 21, 1993 after a long, gallantly fought battle against leukemia. At the time, an effort was underway for his appointment to fill the vacancy of official Vermont Poet. X. J. Kennedy, writer and educator, had already designated him as "the least known major American poet," in an essay appearing in the *Harvard Review*, Winter 1993.]

Index